"LET ME KNOW YOU . . ."

Reflections on Augustine's Search for God

Donald X. Burt, O.S.A.

LITURGICAL PRESS
Collegeville, Minnesota

www.litpress.org

Library of Congress Cataloging-in-Publication Data

Burt, Donald X.
    "Let me know you—" : reflections on Augustine's search for God /
Donald X. Burt.
        p. cm.
    Includes bibliographical references.
    ISBN 0-8146-2957-1 (alk. paper)
    1. Spiritual life—Catholic Church. 2. Augustine, Saint, Bishop of
Hippo. I. Title.
BX2350.3.B87 2003
248.4'82—dc21   2003041636

Contents

Introduction

This prayer was offered by St. Augustine soon after his conversion. He believed that if he could at least understand himself and then discover the path to the vision of God, he would be well on the way to achieving perfect happiness.[1]

Such discovery was not an easy task for him. He spent his first thirty years hiding from himself and devising all sorts of strange images of God. Raised a Christian by his mother Monica, he gradually lost most of his faith except for a fond memory of the story of Jesus Christ. As a young adolescent he was more interested in "fitting in" with his gang than "fitting in" with God. As a young man he was more interested in finding a lovely woman than a loving God.

In his youth he believed that happiness came from physical pleasure and worldly success. It was not until he read the *Hortensius* of Cicero that he began to dream of something more, to dream of finding that elusive understanding of the universe that philosophers call "wisdom." He began to see that there was something beyond ordinary experience that just might explain the turmoil he felt inside himself.

For a time he subscribed to the Manichean belief in a purely material universe that was the battleground for two powerful entities, one good and one evil. They were far different from the personal God he had learned about from his mother. They were not persons at all, just mysterious forces that determined all that happened in the universe. He was a Manichean for nine years, but finally common sense took over. Their mystical description of the world clashed with the empirical science of the day. Despondent, he gave up hope of finding any answers to the ultimate questions about his life and the world in which he lived.

He was rescued from his skepticism by the writings of the Platonic philosophers. He began to see that there could be a world of the "spirit" beyond the everyday world of earthly loves and material comforts. He began to believe that this world was created and controlled by a being who was indeed the "Principle of Good" and that contemplation of this infinite spirit was the goal of human life.

It was only later, through the influence of St. Ambrose, that he learned that this infinite spirit was a person, indeed the God who had walked this earth in the person of Jesus Christ. It took him two more years before he was able to act on this new-found faith, but finally (in his early thirties) he was baptized and committed himself to the Christian way of life. He realized now that God was a God of love and that his destiny was to be united to that God, not by "contemplation" but by "seeing" and "loving." He spent the next forty years trying to expand on that discovery and praying that he would not lose what he had gained so far.

Through his reading of Sacred Scripture he learned that the steps that lead to the "vision" of God had been outlined long before by the Old Testament prophet Isaiah (11:2-3). The first step, *Fear of the Lord*, stands for the darkness in which our journey begins. *Piety* is the next stage, the quiet listening for some direction on how to proceed. Then through increasing *knowledge* we begin to discover who we are and what we need to do to move on. Such awareness of our true "self" and the world in which we must live reveals the imperfections and difficulties in earthly living and leads to the next step where we develop the *fortitude* to continue our journey.

In our continuing confusion we are guided by the gift of *counsel,* which tells us that even in the midst of our bewilderment we can at least practice "loving" by loving those around us, especially by forgiving them the harm they have done to us. As our love deepens and is perfected, we are ready for that final *purification* where we purge ourselves of any remaining attachment to this world. Finally, we come to the end of our journey, the stage of *wisdom.* We are at last prepared to receive the eternal vision of God that awaits us beyond death.

The purpose of the pages that follow is to reflect on these various steps in Augustine's journey toward the vision of God. They were the means by which he finally received the answer to his prayer, "Let me know *you* (O God)!" Perhaps they are also the stages all of us must go through in order to finally "see" the God of love. [2]

Notes

1. Reflections on the search for one's self can be found in *"Let Me Know Myself"* . . . *Reflections on the Prayer of Augustine* (Collegeville: The Liturgical Press, 2002).

2. Unless otherwise indicated, all citations are from the works of St. Augustine. An expanded form of these reflections, including extensive quotes from Augustine, can be found under the title *Loving the Hidden God* on my website: www41.homepage. villanova.edu/donald.burt.

Times of Darkness

1. Darkness

The journey toward union with God, like the journey of life itself, must begin in darkness. The wombed infant, if it is lucky, is propelled by natural forces from its comforting, dark nest into the blazing light of the outside world. Its movement is not a matter of choice. It is not aware of its dark confinement and thus does not voluntarily seek something more. Similarly, once it is thrust into the light of the world outside, it cannot imagine the radiant brilliance that is beyond the surface of its simple life of food and drink and sleep. The infant has yet to think, and thus it cannot dream of the ecstasy of loving and being loved. It has yet to experience the satisfaction of understanding the great truths hidden in reality. It does not yet feel the pride of accomplishment, the joy in the possibility of aiming life at a perfection where all desires will be fulfilled.

As we develop through the various stages of life (childhood, adolescence, maturity, senescence, death), there is a gradual enlightenment but this is usually preceded by new darkness as the next stage in life is anticipated. Indeed, darkness need not wait for the coming of a new age in our lives. It can saturate our lives whenever our usual mode of living is suddenly disrupted by an unexpected event, a condition of life as yet unknown because never before experienced. For example:

- when we are thrust from the comfort of school into the turmoil of the world of work

- when a cherished job is lost
- when retirement is imposed
- when sickness comes
- when death is threatened

Whenever such sudden changes occur, the pleasures of the past seem no longer satisfying. The comfortable, orderly life we had created for ourselves suddenly disappears leaving nothing behind but a vacuum. The accustomed answers by which we ruled our lives seem no longer to apply. We enter a new country and the old maps are of little use.

Some of the darkness that comes into our lives is beyond our control. We cannot avoid being sick. We cannot avoid growing up or growing old or someday dying. But some of the dark periods are self-caused:

- by exuberant expectations that have little to do with the reality of our lives
- by clinging to a past that can never come again
- by hateful acts that drive our loves away
- by a depraved or wasted life that leaves behind undying remorse for what might have been

However the darkness comes upon us, we feel like a child moving from a familiar, lighted room into a room where no light has begun to shine. Suddenly we are petrified. On the brink of a new stage of life, we don't know where we are going. Indeed, we do not even know where we are. We are in a new situation and the lucidity of the past suddenly becomes muddled. We are immersed in *a darkness of absence* where all gods, all prophets, all wisdom seem to have disappeared.

This darkness of absence is a terrible event in anyone's life but it is not as hazardous to our spiritual health as the *darkness of presence*, the darkness that comes from a life lived by false light. Such a condition is like living a life of fantasy in the comforting half-light of a movie theater. Addicted to the show, we do not even realize that we are missing anything. Indeed, if a friend tries to lead us outside into the blazing light of reality, we scream in agony, cover our eyes, and rush back into the comforting darkness inside. Rejoicing in the dim light bathing our dull life, we wish for nothing further. Like a man born blind, we are in darkness and do not realize it. We seek for nothing more. We are like unseeing moles snuffling through a world of underground passages. We are happy with the modest expectations of our murky lives and seek nothing further.

At such dim moments in life, there can occur a therapeutic feeling of emptiness. It is therapeutic because it is the precondition for any movement towards a new state of life. The process of searching for satisfaction must begin with dissatisfaction. If I never sensed the hollowness of my life, I would never feel the need to be "filled up." If I were not dissatisfied with what I have and what I am, I would never reach out for something more.

This dissatisfaction with my condition is sometimes sharpened by a sudden awareness of my contingency, that I am living a life of no great moment and on borrowed time. The pride that I had taken in earthly accomplishments suddenly seems foolish and I begin to look elsewhere for fulfillment. There is a sudden and unexpected development of humility when I recognize that, indeed, I am NOT in charge of the universe, that I do not have all the answers to life and death. It is only then that I may begin to turn away from what was to what might be.

This barren feeling can take various forms. For fervent believers it may take the form of a "Dark Night of the Soul," a sudden disbelief in any God who truly cares about their lives. In the darkness of their newly experienced disbelief, they become convinced that their lives are literally going *no where* because there is no final *where* to go, no place, no condition that will bring that perfect happiness that they so desperately desire. They become convinced that life does not have a goal, only an end. They live out their days and then they die. That's the end of it, and (worst of all) that's the end of *them*.

For the unbeliever, the turning away from the emptiness of their present life may be a turning towards a great unknown.

They humbly accept the fact that they are not in control of their happiness, that the full life they had tried to make for themselves is empty, that they need something more. As was the case with the troubled believer, there is fear but it is not the fear of some vengeful God. The confused believer fears that their life will be punished after death; the searching unbeliever fears that they will finally die forever after a life dimly lived.

Augustine believed that whether we are a confused believer or a despairing nonbeliever, such fear can be the first step in our search for the true, but as yet unknown, God. Though we may live in darkness there is at least some movement in our lives. No longer satisfied with what "is," we are moved to reach out for something more, for something that "might be," to look for some step up from our dark valley. Such fear, as depressing as it may be, can be the beginning of wisdom because wisdom must begin with the acceptance of the fact that we are "not wise," that we do not have all the answers, that indeed we are not God, that we are not the "end-all and be-all" of creation. We are still blind, but now at least we *know* it. That in itself is progress.

2. Blindness

Augustine believed that sight was the most precious sense-power that we humans possess (*Commentary on Psalm 26/2*, 8). It was a constant joy for him to savor the sight of the beautiful land and sky and sea that surrounded him in the lush land of North Africa. It was truly a splendid thing to know that he had friends, but it was even better to be able to see them, to have them present, and behold the affection shining from their eyes. In the midst of his various physical problems, he praised God for allowing him to continue to see. Better by far to be poor and seeing than to be rich and blind.

Perhaps blindness is less of a burden for those who, like Bartimaeus in the Gospel story (Mark 10:46-52), were born blind. Never experiencing sight, they do not know what they are missing. Blind from infancy, they respond like every other infant, adjusting to the life that has been given to them. Only later, when they begin to compare themselves to others and hear others tell them what they are missing, will they perhaps weep for their loss and feel cheated.

The adjustment is more difficult for those who have experienced sight and then become blind. Once you have experienced the light of the sun, it is harder to live in the darkness of a moonless night. So too for the blindness of the spirit that sometimes comes unexpectedly as we move through life. In such spiritual blindness we feel shut off from that divine light that used to guide us from within (*Commentary on Psalm 6*, 8). The effect of suddenly plunging from enlightened ecstasy into dark depression is truly dreadful. It is a shock to suddenly "not know where you are going" after being so sure that everything in your life was just fine. Your life has taken a sudden turn and your are not prepared for it.

Certainly none of us are prepared for the trauma of existence. To move from "nothing" to "something" is indeed a radical change. Perhaps that is why we all seem to be born with clouded vision. It is as though we begin our existence with cataracts of the spirit, living a grey life in a universe of brilliant color, depending on the words of others to tell us what the world is like, depending on the words of others to give us hope. Thus, in our first years we were told to "eat our dinner" so that we could grow big and strong, but we really did not know for sure how that could happen and how it would feel to be big and strong. As young teens we were told to go to school and study hard so that we could gain an important place in the world. But in our teens it was sometimes hard to believe that anyone would ever think we were important, that there indeed was a significant place for us in the unknown world that lay ahead.

This need to plunge into the unknown future continued through life. When we were young we were assured that someday we would find a true love, but before it happened it was hard to know what the experience of love would be like, or to believe that someday it would come to us. In the prime of our lives, we were told that we could indeed have a grand old age if we prepared for it, if we took care of ourselves, if we invested wisely, if we bought the right insurance. But there was no insurance that our "golden years" would indeed be golden. We could not know before the fact whether we would grow old gracefully or indeed whether we would ever grow old.

When we get sick, when we are dying, inevitably there will be kind souls who will assure us that some day we will be well, that someday we will live grand lives free forever from the threat of death. We truly want to believe it, but before it happens it is so hard to see what vibrant health and life beyond death really is and to believe that it will really happen to us. Like Bartimaeus we, too, are blind and cannot see what lies ahead. We know that our lives are moving but where they are going we simply do not know. People have told us of the good things that await us and we have fervently wanted to believe them, but in our dark days of blindness, it seems improbable (if not impossible) that we will ever see again.

The saving factor in the life of the blind Bartimaeus was that he never gave up hope. After a life lived in darkness, being pushed here and there by those who could supposedly see, being supported by the pity of others, he never gave up hope that one day he would be able to see the world as it is. Bartimaeus had to spend many years in darkness before he finally could see. So too, as we go through the periods of darkness in our lives, all we can do is to put up with our blindness and wait for the light to come. Our consolation in our blindness can come only through the belief that, although Christ may not come quickly with a cure, this is not a sign that he is distant. The story of Bartimaeus teaches us that Jesus is with the blind even when he does not make all things clear.

The story of the blind Bartimaeus ends happily. Jesus opened his eyes, and for the first time he could see. The happy man put behind him the memories of his past blindness and, now seeing clearly, began to follow Jesus down the road that led to the land beyond time, Jesus' eternal city where the "Son" always shines and everyone can see just fine.

3. Great Expectations

One of the reasons for our sometime periods of darkness is that we expect too much. It is in our nature to seek infinity even as we are suffocated by the finite. We are limited beings created with a thirst for the unlimited. We are dependent beings who wish we could depend on no one but ourselves. We are beings destined to die, who want to live forever.

Considered just by itself, this opposition between what we are now and what we want to be may seem to be a cruel joke, but within the context of the Christian faith this tension is an expression of God's highest love for human beings. We were created finite because that's the best God could do. Even God was limited by possibility, and it was simply impossible to have a world in which two "infinite" beings existed. But it was possible to create a finite being with a chance (through the help of God) of eventually being united to the Infinite through love. This is precisely what God did.

But is this not cruel? Is it not similar to creating a person without legs who has a passion to run? Is it not like creating a person without eyes who desperately wants to see? Certainly it would be cruel to give someone an intense desire that is impossible to satisfy, but our desire for the infinite is *not* impossible. Even though we are undoubtedly finite, it is still possible to have our desire for the infinite fulfilled. Our great expectation of possessing infinite good is not a curse but our greatest gift, a gift which drives us forward by making us dissatisfied with the limited good that we are able to achieve here on earth.

Now that I am in my "geezer-hood," I have come to see that having too many great expectations about *this* life can indeed be a curse. Our expectations for the joys of eternal life are warranted. Our expectation for a life on earth filled with such perfect joy is one source of the recurrent darkness in our lives. When we expect too much, we can never be satisfied with the limited but fine goods that we actually possess.

It is hard to avoid the temptation to expect too much as we make our way through life. In every stage of our living, we have great expectations. Being alive seems to breed optimism; it is only through experienced disasters that we become pessimists. In our baby days we expected everything good and waited impatiently for the amazing future that we just *knew* would be better than our happy present. If as infants we had a fair share of love and comfort (and sadly some babies do not realize even that modest expectation), we could not even imagine that there was anything bad in the days ahead. We were friends with the universe. We had to be taught the sad truth that we should not talk to strangers nor play with foreign dogs nor cross busy streets unattended. In those early days we rejoiced in that first great gift of God: life itself. Even before we could put it into words our laughter shouted: "I am alive and life is good!"

Our first years were like a repetition of the days of Eden when humans walked as friends with God and had nothing to fear and much to look forward to. We even had an advantage over Adam and Eve in that we could not make mistakes. We were too little to be too bad. Whatever blemishes darkened our lives were inherited from others. All too soon those flaws began to reveal themselves. We began to expect too much from those around us. Even before we had words, we began to cry out to get our own way.

When we grew out of infancy to become little kids, our selfishness became more conscious. Like young colts unwillingly imprisoned by halters imposed by others and led away in directions we did not choose, we were sent to school. Beginning school, our great expectation for a free and unfettered life was crushed. We had to face the reality that the world expected us to *know* something and to *do* something worthwhile with that knowledge. They cried: "Make *something* of yourself!" ignoring the fact that we were already *someone*.

Having survived the perils of "growing up," we began the flourishing days of our youth, and our expectations grew even larger. After all, we were young and strong. The future seemed to be in our hands. We thought we could make ourselves anything we wanted to be. We looked forward to becoming a success, finding people who would like us (or at least *respect* us), hoping that we would find someone somewhere who would love us, be friends with us, perhaps even share their lives with us.

Of course, our expectations were not without fear. We knew that life was not perfect, that it was possible to fail, that it was possible to love and not be loved. Whereas as a small child we thought ourselves to be just lovely and the center of the universe, now we knew better. In the midst of our search for love, we may have even begun to hate ourselves, to try to become what we thought others wanted us to: fatter, thinner, smarter, "cooler." We quickly discovered that this was a tragic mistake. As Adam and Eve discovered to their sorrow, expectations can only be fulfilled if they flow from what we truly *are*.

In our middle years we looked ahead and perhaps began to worry about our shortened future. There was diminished time to do what we wanted to do and diminished energy to fight the conflicting currents of our lives. But at the same time we now had an established life, an accustomed way of living, an accustomed work, an accustomed love; and, if we were happy with what we had achieved, we could look forward with great expectation to a retirement that gave us time to relax and enjoy the fruits of our life, surrounded by those whose love for us had been proven over time. But, as we all know, such happy plans do not always work out.

When we are very old, our expectations become quite modest, but they still may be too extravagant for the actual condition of our lives. We hope that we will not have great pain or be a great pain to others. We hope to have a loved one by our side. We hope that our passing will be with some sort of dignity. But, again as we know, such dreams are sometimes unfulfilled.

When our future grows short, there is no room for long-range expectations about this life. We are close to the death that marks the end of our time. Most of this life exists only in memory, and our expectations must now become focused on the life that awaits us after death. We must continue to fight against desires about this life that go far beyond what is possible. In expecting too much from our waning days, we plunge ourselves into a despair caused by hopes that can never be fulfilled. We become unable to enjoy what we have, those gifts given to us in the providence of God to help us attain the joys beyond death, joys that we cannot expect because they are so far beyond our earthly imagination.

4. The Darkness of Despair

At one point in his early life, Augustine seems to have been overcome by despair. He was at the low point in his life. The paradox was that he was a young and healthy man with a prosperous future ahead of him. His career was taking off. He was surrounded by family and friends who seemed to love him. Yet he felt that his life had no meaning. He could not find that vision of himself and the world that would give him a direction in life. He despaired of ever making true sense of his life, of ever finding a God whom he could believe in and depend on.

Augustine's experience shows that despair can come to us even in the so-called "good times" of our lives. Sometimes it is precisely at that moment when we seem to have everything to live for that we begin to doubt deep in our hearts that life is worth living. Sometimes despair is an unwelcome guest at birthday parties and family gatherings. Indeed, it is not unknown in communities of religious men and women.

Just as happiness depends on the fulfillment of our basic desires for life, love, meaning, and freedom, so despair sometimes follows when we think that any one of these will never be fulfilled. I have heard of perfectly healthy people with important positions in life and the fullness of freedom who take their lives because they thought that their life had *no meaning*. A friend of mine with a good job and loving family committed suicide the day after he discovered that he had cancer. For him death seemed to be a better alternative than an *ebbing life*. The mother of another friend of mine who was an only child seemed to waste away after he died. Life lost all meaning for her without *someone to love*. Prisoners have been known to choose death rather than prison. The loss of life seemed preferable to *loss of freedom*. Indeed, I suspect that sometimes despair grows out of simple *boredom with living*. Like the character in the story told by Sartre, we are tempted to plunge a knife not through our hand but through our heart, just to have an experience of something different.

When you think about it, the human temptation to despair is understandable. We have a thirst for the perfect, for the eternal, but we must live out these days in a world that is an imperfect fading world. We have a natural need to "wonder" at the world, to discover new and interesting things, to have new and exciting experiences, but our lives have become a succession of "*same-old*" "*same-old*" days. We are in a rut and we fear that it will gradually widen into a grave that will hold us till the end of time.

As we have observed in the previous thoughts on "Great Expectations," our despair can flow from unrealistic delusions about ourselves and the world in which we live. We are born with wonderful expectations for a world that will be just fantastic and when we discover that those expectations will be difficult to realize, we sometimes become morose. The laughter of our infant days is followed by the tears of a flawed life, one necessarily falling short of our wish for a bright world filled with happiness.

Despair can make our life on earth a living hell. It can also make us begin to doubt God. We forget that our faith does not promise a heaven on earth, but only that God will put us on the road to heaven and will give us his grace to help us on the way. Despair makes us doubt that promise; it may even stop all progress.

In the midst of such despair, we must be careful that we don't *stumble and fall* by succumbing to some new perversity, some new addiction. We tumble from that high stairway to heaven that we had built so laboriously for ourselves by leading virtuous lives. There is the danger, then, that we will have no inclination to pick ourselves up and start over. We may forget that we live in a world where it will always be necessary to say, "I'm sorry!" again and again. We may forget that although we are "renewed in Christ," we still are cracked and that those cracks will manifest themselves again and again in unexpected ways. If we take our fall too seriously, we may react like a sick person suddenly diagnosed with a terminal disease, saying to ourselves:

> What's the use? Why fight any longer for good health? Let me now indulge in all those destructive habits that I fought against for so many years. Let me eat what I want and drink to excess and begin again to look for love wherever I can find it. And please don't try to stop me by warning that these habits will endanger my life! I am already a member of the living dead, one who has no hope for salvation in this life or the next!

Our despair has made us *"fall off the road."*

Our faith tells us that the path to heaven is definite and fixed. It is the way outlined for us by Jesus Christ and it consists in living a moral life centered on love, realizing that our successes depend on the grace of God. No one can stay on this path if they are too proud or too despairing. Other moral faults may slow our progress but at least we are still on the road. We may be "back-sliding" but at least we are still on the path, and there is always the chance that we will follow the example of the Prodigal Son and turn around when our wandering life turns sour. But if we have created our own imaginary road to perfection through pride or have fallen into the crevasse of despair and make no effort to remedy our situation, then we will be lost forever unless some miracle of grace pulls us down from our self-created pinnacle or lifts us out of the pit.

Even if we don't fall from the road, our despair may cause us to be "stuck in place," to become completely absorbed by present trivialities or nostalgia for the past. We think that we and the world are spinning towards a future that is even worse than the present. It seems better to just concentrate on the present and make it as pleasant as possible even if it means "not thinking" about it by immersing ourselves in the pleasures and fantasies of the moment.

Or we may spend our time reminiscing about the "good *old* days," those historic times when life seemed simpler and heroes and romance ruled the world, those grand days when we were young and life was an adventure, days when perhaps we were held in the arms of a lovely beloved who is now gone. It is indeed foolish to long for the *idyllic past,* which can never return. If we ever thought about them seriously, we would realize that they were no better than the present. They are idyllic only in that they are true "idylls of the mind," a fantasy appropriate to poetry but not reality.

Augustine goes so far as to suggest that the reason why these fantasies of the past seem so attractive is because they never existed. They are not "what was" but "what we would have liked to have been" (*Sermon 25*, 3). It is easy to idealize a past that you have never experienced, to become rhapsodic about the glories of outdoor plumbing when you were never forced to use it. To think that the past was a *utopia* filled with good times has in itself a hidden truth. As the meaning of the word itself suggests, such perfect times are to be found in "no place."

The sad thing about many of our days of despair is that they may come from simple weariness. We have not *fallen* on the road to heaven, we have just *become tired*. We have tried to live a good life, but now we are infected with the terrible temptation of the virtuous: boredom in leading a good life (*Commentary on Psalm 106*, 6). We see that the road ahead seems dark and long and we say to ourselves: "Why not just sit here in the fading light of my life and dream of days when all was bright and a happy life seemed possible?"

The apathy and nostalgia that flow from despair about anything better *down* the road makes us sit down *on* the road. Rather than move in the wrong direction, we just squat and mope. The beginning of our climb out of the depths of despair is to cry out for help. As Augustine told his friend: "Those who can cry out from the abyss are not in the very depths of the abyss. Their very cry lifts them up" (*Commentary on Psalm 39*, 3). But to do even this demands grace from God and great courage from us in order that we might at least begin to hope for hope. Here being a Christian is a distinct advantage because if we have just a little faith in the words and deeds of Jesus Christ, we can listen to and be encouraged by Paul's words: "Who will separate us from the love of Christ? Can trial, or distress, or hunger, or persecution, or nakedness, or danger, or the sword sweep us away? We can conquer all of these because of the power of the love that Christ has showered on us" (Rom 8:35-37). Believing in such assurances, we can begin again to hope.

5. Hope in Darkness

Despair follows from the realization that the times are bad and are unlikely to get any better, that the circumstances of one's life will always be irremediably unsatisfactory. It is understandable that people will sometimes try to escape life when they perceive that the human environment, the cruelty and anger and hate they see all around them, is simply part of the human condition and that nothing can be done about it. Such sensitive souls cry out, "I cannot live here any more," and try to move on to something else, either a supposedly "better" life or simply the nonlife of oblivion. For them oblivion seems a better alternative to living in conditions without hope.

Augustine was convinced that we must have hope in *something* to get through this life (*Sermon 158*, 8). Even if life is painful, we can keep plodding along as long as we see the possibility of relief in the future. We are like small children nearly exhausted as they trudge along the hot streets of a seashore town on their way to the ocean. If they have hope of eventually plunging into the cool waters of the distant sea, they keep plodding along. If hope disappears, they give up and refuse to go any farther.

God, of course, could arrange our lives so that hope would not be necessary. We would then possess what we wanted, not pine for it. The reason why God does not give us the "good life" is obvious. If life were always sweet, who would ever want to move on? (*Sermon 346A*, 8). We might begin to think that the purpose of faith is to give constant ecstasy in life rather than to get us through it with some nobility (*City of God* 22.22.4). Furthermore, hope for what we do not have expands us, getting us beyond this cramped life that we lead day by day. Through hope we begin to dream of worlds never seen, of loves yet to be found, of great works yet to be accomplished. In sum, hope draws us out of our pedestrian present and encourages us to fly (*Commentary on the First Epistle of John*, 4.6).

Especially for one who believes the message of Jesus Christ, there are many good reasons for hope despite the trials of life. First, this life is not as bad as we sometimes make it out to be. Augustine certainly had his good days and bad days, but even in the midst of his bad days he was able to have hope because of his belief that God was near. He was not so naive as to believe that bad times would never come. Indeed, his own experience contradicted that fantasy.

After the turmoil of his early years, after losing a son and mother and friends in death, after spending his life to make North Africa Christian (only to die with barbarians pounding on the gates of his city), after a series of real (or imagined) illnesses, Augustine was not about to deny that bad things happen to good and bad people alike. For him this life was more like an oil-press than a vacation spa. It was a place for purifying the good and identifying the bad. Sometimes pressure comes from natural disasters; at other times, from the malice of human beings. However it comes, it challenges the good to come to the top and forces the bad into the depths. As in a goldsmith's furnace, the gold would never be purified if the straw were not burnt up (*Sermon 113A*, 11).

As we search for good times there is a need, day by day, to simply get through the times that are not so good. In such times our hope can come from the same source that gave hope to Augustine: the conviction that whatever happens to us we are not alone, that there is a Divine *Someone* standing by our side ready and willing and able to help us endure. Wherever we wander in space and time the words of Paul remain true: ". . . the Lord is near. Do not be anxious about anything" (Phil 4:5-6).

The good news is that God does not discriminate in granting his presence. He is equally present to and present in rich and poor, men and women, young and old (*Sermon 47*, 30). Indeed, he is present to the sinner as well as the saint. God may be ignored but he will never depart. He remains, willing to reveal himself if asked. Anyone who turns back to him will find him in their hearts (*Confessions 5. 2*). God will come and dwell in anyone who does not reject him out of hand. He is not too proud to come to even the most humble (*Sermon 23*, 6). And more, not only is Christ with us now on earth, in some mysterious way we are with him even now in heaven. He is here on earth through his compassionate charity; we are in heaven through our hope-filled love (*Commentary on Psalm 122*, 1).

No matter how bad or good this life may be, we have an added reason for hope in that we have been promised that we shall live forever and that we have it within our power to make that eternal life a happy one. There can be absolutely no doubt that what has been promised will happen because it is Jesus-God himself who has promised it (*Commentary on Psalm 122*, 9). Christ has promised that, although we cannot control how we shall die, we can choose to live a good life and living in that way we can be sure that our life beyond death will be happy.

Granted that we can achieve a happy eternal life if we live a good life in time, how can we live such a life considering our obvious confusion and weaknesses? Here too our hope rests on a promise, the promise that God will give the grace to live a good life and the forgiveness to cleanse a life that is not so good.

Of course, it would be foolish to believe that we will never fail. Our first day in a health club does not guarantee that we will be suddenly strong. The flab of years is not dissolved in a day, but to despair of ever being strong would be self-defeating. Even the great heroes of the Old and New Testaments had their ups and downs. Paul was converted by being knocked off his "high horse" but this did not mean that he would thereafter be preserved from every "sting of the flesh." Even the great Moses alternated between failure and strength. At the Red Sea he needed two others to help keep his arms raised so that the chosen people could have safe passage. Is it likely that the same God who supported Moses in his great adventure will desert any of us as we make our way to our own promised land? (*Sermon 252, 6*).

If we do fail from time to time, there is no question that our sins will be forgiven if we ask. God is not seeking proud perfection, only humble contrition. If he did not want to heal us, he could have easily put us out of our misery. As it is, the fact that we are still alive is a sign that the Divine Doctor has not given up on us.

Therefore, we always have reason for hope even in our days of darkness. God has not left us alone; he is still active in our lives. Indeed, sometimes our darkness is a divine grace that is pushing us beyond our accustomed way of living by revealing the futility of the alternative we have chosen. Recognizing the vanity of our life, we (like a drowning man in a filthy stream), begin to reach out for *any* relief from the stagnation and pollution of our present condition. Finally, aware of the emptiness of our present lives, we are ready to sit quietly and wait for direction. Convinced of our inability to find the answers to our changing lives ourselves, we wait for guidance from powers beyond us. In our darkness we are ready to climb to the next stage in our search for God. We enter a time of *piety*, where we patiently *listen* for someone to tell us what we should do next.

2

Pious Listening

1. Listening

The second step in our journey toward God is a period of *pious listening*. Piety is a gift of the Holy Spirit through which we are able to develop a meek and docile demeanor, patiently waiting for some guidance in choosing what we should do with our futures. We humbly accept the fact that we do not have all the answers to life's questions, and we look to the still unseen God for direction. Augustine believed that the best example of such patient listening was the heroic Job described in the Old Testament, sitting quietly after losing most of what mattered to him, refusing to condemn God or anyone else, waiting for guidance, ready to yield to the will of God whatsoever it might command (*Sermon 157*, 2). He also believed that those who are able to endure with hope this period of patient listening are like the "blessed meek" spoken of in the beatitudes (*Commentary on the Sermon on the Mount*, 1.4.11).

Such periods of pious listening gave Augustine an openness to new possibilities throughout his long life. He came to recognize that God could speak to humans in many different ways, sometimes through the needs of a beloved spouse or child, sometimes through the exigencies of time and place, sometimes through the loud demands of the people of God, sometimes through the call of the Church, sometimes through the advice of friends, sometimes through the accusations of enemies. With the help of St. Ambrose, he learned that the most important source of divine revelation was the Sacred Scriptures.

He also learned (by experience) that it takes a truly docile mind to hear and act on the message hidden in the sacred writings (*Commentary on the Sermon on the Mount*, 1.3.10).

Docility is obviously required when we *don't understand* the message. At such a time all we can do is to humbly accept that the words sometimes contain great mysteries that perhaps will never be understood or (at best) can be understood only after a long period of study. If we are truly dedicated to pious listening, we will not reject out-of-hand truths that we think absurd at first reading. We will not reject the teaching on the Trinity because we cannot understand how God can be one and yet three. We will not reject the mystery of the Incarnation because we cannot understand how Jesus can be both human and divine. Our docility allows us to see that it is not the truth of the teaching that is the obstacle; it is our own limited powers of knowing.

Docility is also required when we *do understand* what Scripture is telling us to do but we find the command unpleasant. If the inspired words are clearly telling us to change our way of life, we may angrily proclaim that our own ("easier") plans for our lives make more sense than the "hard saying" we hear from the sacred writings (*Christian Doctrine*, 2.7.9). In his early years Augustine found it difficult to develop such docility. Comfortable with his life, he feared any radical change. In his late teens he had read Cicero's *Hortensius* and discovered that there was a world beyond the world of earthy pleasures, the world of a *wisdom* that could be acquired only by living a more spiritual life. Ten years later we find him still vacillating. By this time he had rediscovered Christ, but he was still unwilling to make the whole-hearted conversion of life to the "wisdom" that his convictions demanded (*Confessions*, 8.7.17). It took him two more years before he was able to accept and act on those convictions and be baptized.

Of course, understanding (and even not understanding) the message presupposes that we first have *heard* it, and this in itself is a problem. As we live out our lives in this hurlyburly world, it is increasingly difficult to find a quiet place where we can listen to the quiet words of God directing us. God is heard only in times of peaceful silence, but to achieve such quiet stillness seems almost impossible for us living embedded as we are in the confusion of everyday living. We are swept along by the conflicting currents of our times.

Far from hearing quiet "words" soothing the discordant disruption of our days, we hear too many words. We are surrounded by NOISE, suffocated by shouting voices screaming endlessly about what God is like, what God hates, who is evil and who is good, who is damned and who is saved, quoting Scripture passages out of context, emphasizing this word or that, "talking heads" never shutting up, running on forever and ever . . . (as I am doing here).

Augustine once told a friend that he thought it easier to bear the difficulties and storms of the wilderness than the things humans must suffer or fear in the "busyness" of the world (*Letter 95*, 4). To another he wrote, "I simply cannot taste and enjoy the truly good things of eternity as long as I have no relief from the care and work of today" (*Letter 10*, 2). What he was saying was that all of us must find our own quiet hermitage to listen to God's voice, and the only place where this exists in this noisy world is within our own selves. Only in this hidden, quiet place can we find a personal solitude hidden from everyone else. Outside, the world is driven "hither and yon" by storms and troubles. It is only inside that we can reflect on the meaning of our life and death, ponder God and ourselves, examine our loves and hates. It is only there that we can find peaceful rest and in that quiet rest rediscover hope. It is a secret place where only we and God dwell, a place where God can reveal to us what we have hidden even from ourselves.

It is hard for any human being to achieve this quiet. The uproar of the world keeps calling us from our inner sanctuaries, demanding that we look back to this world rather than look forward to the world to come (*Sermon 105*, 5.7). The more we become attached to the noisy world outside, the more we may come to fear withdrawing to the silence within, frightened that it will become a prison from which we cannot escape. Only through a habit of quiet solitude can we come to see it for what it is, an Eden with no walls, a world of reverie where anything is possible, a safe place where for a while we can sit and watch the noisy world outside, a place where at last we can hear the soft voice of the Divine Teacher within.

2. The Divine Teacher

In his *Confessions* (9.10.25), Augustine tried to describe the indescribable: standing face to face with God and hearing his voice speaking directly without intermediary. He and his mother seemed to have had an instant of such contact, a mystical experience in which mother and son for a brief moment stood face to face with the Father-God of us all. Of course, it did not last. The silence necessary to hear God through such immediate contact was soon disrupted and from the heavens both fell back to earth. As far as we know neither had an experience as intense as this again. Monica soon died and Augustine spent the next forty years trying to bring the reality of God to people embroiled in the confusion and noise of everyday living. Monica through her death received the permanent vision of God. Augustine for the rest of his earthly life was left with only a memory.

Still, the memory brought with it the conviction that God still spoke to him now from deep inside his very self. He became convinced through his faith and through his experience that Christ dwells within every human and that for every human he was the most important teacher, a teacher who reveals truths about the world by illuminating humans with his presence, a teacher who speaks to each person about themselves through their conscience. Throughout his long life Augustine returned again and again to the theme that the words of human preachers and teachers were useless if those listening would not listen to the quiet words of the God within.

He told those who crowded around him seeking answers to questions about the meaning of life:

> We have Jesus our teacher inside each one of us. If you can't understand what I am saying, listen to the Christ who is in your hearts. It is this Christ who gives me the words to say and it is this Christ who will reveal deep inside your own "self" the message he wants you to get through hearing my words (*Commentary on the Gospel of John*, 20.3).

The people he preached to over his lifetime had a need to be inspired by God, but it was not because they were more ignorant or stupid than the rest of the human race. Augustine assured them that their need to listen carefully to the "Divine Teacher Within" was a need for every human being no matter how skillful they might be in theology, no matter how noble a position they held in the Church. He made this point very clearly one day in a sermon to the people in his congregation, telling them:

> My friends, all of us stand before the same Divine Teacher as fellow pupils. The fact that we bishops speak to you from this high podium does not make us your teachers. The Divine One who lives in each of us is the Teacher for us all (*Sermon 134*, 1).

How this internal teacher speaks to us during the ordinary days of our lives is as much a mystery as mystical experience itself. God seems to communicate with us through our day-by-day experiences of the world or through ideas that suddenly "pop up" in our head (*City of God*, 16.6). In both cases we hear a God who speaks from within our very selves. The words of humans or the events occurring in the created universe are but the occasions for the Divine Teacher to reveal the truth hidden in the words or events. Just as the sounds of the voice of the preacher resounding outside us cause the delicate membrane of our ear to vibrate and carry the message inside through the thin barrier of flesh, so the whisper of God pierces the even more slender membrane that separates time and eternity in the depths of our soul. The touch of God's voice deep inside causes our souls to resonate in tandem, and suddenly we know the truth that he wants us to recognize, a truth that goes far beyond the simple words of the teacher who speaks to us from outside.

One thing is certain: the place of God is inside us, and it is through the "ears" of our spirits that he speaks to us. When we come to understand the truths hidden in the universe and to believe the truths taught by our faith, the avenue of revelation is our own minds. Perhaps the message was first proclaimed by some human being, but once inside the listener it was *illuminated* by the light of the Divine Teacher. It is through such illumination more than the power of the words coming from outside, that we come to say to ourselves: "Indeed, I understand and it is TRUE!" The function of the human teacher who instructs us is not so much to communicate a truth as it is to "not get in the way" of the illumination of the God who teaches deep within the listener.

In the case of truths about ourselves, unpleasant truths that demand correction, pleasing truths that give hope, inspirations that call us to some new way of serving God and working out our salvation, the instrument of communication is again our minds, now acting in their function as conscience. Sometimes the truths revealed here are the most difficult to accept because they say something about our own lives and perhaps challenge us to change. We fight against the message. Rather than desiring to follow out what we hear, we try to hear what we desire to hear (*Confessions*, 10.26.37).

This reaction against the truth does not normally occur when the truth is some obscure fact about the universe. No one that I know has become emotionally upset by the discovery of the rules of geometry. In these areas that do not pertain directly to us, we accept the truths and move on with our lives. Our reaction is often quite different when the truths are truths about ourselves, truths that perhaps we have been avoiding for years, truths like:

- I am selfish!
- I am proud!
- I am constantly plagued by my passions!
- I have a destructive addiction!

It is difficult to hear such harsh truths even though they may have been sounding in our internal ears for years. We have known what we are in some vague way, but we have avoided listening too intently lest we face the unpleasant conclusion that our lives are somewhat of a mess and that we must do something to crawl out of our comfortable mire. It is much easier to stand before the world and cry "I understand geometry," than to stand and hear the truth of the words about ourselves sounding deep inside, words that no one outside has perhaps dared to say to us about our vices and weaknesses.

These truths about ourselves are terribly difficult to accept but they are also terribly important. I can be saved (Thank God!) without knowing too much geometry; but I cannot be saved and thereby see God if I avoid the truths about myself that God is whispering to me deep inside. Thus, the counsel of Augustine to us (whatever our status or stage of life may be) is well-advised:

> Let us leave a little room for reflection in our lives. Let us leave room for periods of silence. Let us enter into ourselves; let us leave behind all noise and confusion. Let us look within ourselves and see whether there is some delightful hidden place in our consciousness where we can be free of noise and argument, where we need not be carrying on our disputes and planning to have our own stubborn way. Let us hear the Word of God in stillness and perhaps we may come to understand (*Sermon 52*, 22).

3. The Need for an Open Mind

There is no use pretending to sit quietly and listen piously to the Divine Teacher within if we do not listen with an open mind, a mind that is receptive to any message that is given even if it is disturbing. It is not an easy thing to do. As Augustine observes, when the inside of our "houses" (our inner selves) are disordered we will use any excuse to stay outdoors (*Commentary on Psalm 22/2*, 8).

Of course, it is impossible to have a completely open mind. There is an axiom from philosophy that states: *Omnis recipitur secundum modum recipientis,* that is, "All that is received by a hearer is received according to the circumstances of the hearer." The principle points to the common-sense truth that if you pour water into a cylinder it will take the form of the cylinder. If you pour it into a rectangular tub, it will appear rectangular. If you pour it into a vessel with a faulty bottom, it will rush through with no lasting effect. So too the messages received and understood by our minds are formed and shaped by the quality of our knowing powers and by our histories.

Each of us listens and understands messages a bit differently. Knowledge is not a process where all the listeners are like homologous wax waiting patiently to receive exactly the same imprint from a common experience. We are not ponds of soft wax but pools of living spirit, amorphous globs created individually and separately and then shaped and molded by the different events of our lives, our histories, our actions, and reactions to the stimuli of the world inside and outside our inner selves.

Our different perceptions of these internal and external worlds provide the raw material that the Divine Teacher uses to reveal the truths that we need to know to achieve our eternal destiny. As Augustine frequently told his listeners, we may all *hear* the same words but we *understand* them in our own way. The old story of the blind men asked to describe an elephant illustrates this fact. The one who held the trunk thought the elephant was like a snake. The one who embraced the leg thought it was like a tree. The one who felt its side thought it was like a wall. The one who held its tail thought it was like a vine. In each case what they said was true, but their experiences were too narrow to see the whole truth, that the elephant was everything they said and something much more. Their narrow judgments were influenced by their condition in life, their blindness, and their place by the elephant. So too when we listen for the truth about reality, we may hear part of the truth, but it will always be incomplete. Only God can see the whole picture.

This is why the Divine Teacher does his teaching from inside each of us, showing us the truth that is important for us at that particular moment in our lives. Because of Augustine's belief in the Divine Teacher within each of us, he was not surprised that different human beings could read the same passage of Sacred Scripture and take a meaning from it that was different for each, indeed even different from the intention of the writer (*Confessions*, 12.18). For example, the story of Jesus curing the blind man may be an interesting event to someone who can see, but to a blind person it is a message of hope. Those who are involved in an adulterous relationship may read the story of the woman who was guilty of adultery but was forgiven by Jesus as an encouragement to turn their lives around. For the confessor innocent of that sin (but guilty of many others), it should be a lesson on how to deal with penitents who come to the Sacrament of Reconciliation asking forgiveness.

Augustine himself, before his own conversion to Christianity, was influenced dramatically by two stories. The first story came through a conversation with his friend Simplicianus. It described the conversion of Victorinus (an intellectual like Augustine) who had much to lose by public proclamation of his faith but who had conquered his fear and bravely proclaimed it. For many who heard the story, it was just a story, but for Augustine it was a message which filled him with enthusiasm to follow Victorinus' example (*Confessions*, 8.5). The second story was told to him by another friend, Ponticianus. It had to do with the hermit, Anthony, who had turned his back on the things of this world to pursue God with his whole heart (*Confessions*, 8.6). Once again, for many others it was just a story, but the special message Augustine heard was life-changing. He listened with an open mind, ready to receive the message God had for him, and the message he heard changed the direction of his life. Up to that point in his life, he had turned his back on himself, refusing to see himself as he really was. But, as he listened to the stories about these two good men, he was turned around by the Divine Teacher within and forced finally to look honestly at himself (*Confessions*, 8.7.16).

To hear the message that God is sending to us in the midst of our quiet listening, we must be open to whatever it says, even if it tells us to do something extremely difficult. It is not an easy thing to listen in those circumstances. It is hard to sit quietly in a soiled life and accept the command of the God within to look honestly at that life and deal with it. It is hard to sit quietly and listen to a message that we have been avoiding for years, a message to accept a new way of life that has never before been considered and has about it all of the frightening aspects of the unknown. It is hard to sit quietly and listen to God's whisper deep inside telling us over and over again:

- You do not have all the answers; listen to others, seek guidance!

- The one whom you supposed was to be the love of your life does not love you; move on!

- Your mind and your intentions are not as pure as you pretend. You *do* lust! You *do* hate! You *are* addicted to things that will destroy you! Be conscious of your weakness and fight against it!

- You will not live much longer; you must make preparations to die well so that you can live well eternally!

It is no good to excuse our perversions by saying: "Well, I only *think* such things! I would never do them! I would never kill those I hate! I would never abuse those whom I lust after!" As Augustine warns, God judges evil not simply by deeds done but also by perverse thoughts entertained (*Sermon 170*, 3). Our hidden aberrant tendencies may not get us arrested, but they may close our ears to the internal teacher's shouted warning: "Don't be complacent! You are not as good as you think you are!" Externally we may seem to lead quiet lives worthy of respect but inside we may still relish desires that are not fit to be seen. The law tells us not to lust after another's goods (be it their property or their spouse) and as long as we *covet* them but don't *grab* them, the world thinks of us as splendid people. But inside, where we nurture inflamed desires for the person or property of others, we are not as noble as we sometimes pretend to be (*Sermon 170*, 5).

Certainly none of us who have lived any length of days has a completely unblemished conscience. If we are honest with ourselves, there will always be a tinge of guilt for past evils freely chosen. For all of us with any residue of passion, there will be occasional embarrassing desires that escape arrest only because they are not acted out. We may still feel moments of carnal craving in the presence of some sexually attractive "other." We may still have moments of pride-filled hurt feelings that bubble with eruptions of envy, anger, and desire for revenge. Of course, when we look inside our selves, there are usually some good things to be found too, but the bad we find seems to capture our attention more. Perhaps it is because when you slog through a swamp it is difficult to appreciate the clear blue sky above.

It may be charity to hide a truth from another, fearing that it may destroy them. It is kindness sometimes to go along with a dying loved one's fantasy that soon they will be better. But it is stupidity to refuse to listen to a disturbing truth about ourselves. In the search for our real selves, ignorance is not bliss. It is foolishness. We are what we are whether or not we face up to it. Attempting to lie about ourselves to God goes beyond foolishness. It is insanity. God already has the truth about us, and the only reason why God wants us to admit that truth (be it bad or good) is for our benefit. When you think about it, the reason why we are sometimes unable to say "I'm sorry!" is not because we are worried about shocking the Divine Teacher. Rather it is because we do not want to admit our malice to ourselves. Once proclaimed we can no longer ignore it; we are forced to do something about it.

Perhaps this is part of the therapy of the Sacrament of Reconciliation. In speaking our sins anonymously to another human being, we are not exposing our selves to that other person so much as exposing our warts and wounds to ourselves. In confessing we no longer avoid the bad parts of being ourselves, we hang them out for us to see and in that action demonstrate our sorrow more powerfully than any words can express. God must smile when we make such confessions because he knows that knowledge is the beginning of contrition and that contrition is the beginning of salvation. He can then forgive us because we have taken the first step in forgiving ourselves. We are no longer playing the game "Liar! Liar!" and have finally moved away from fantasy to reality. We have opened our minds and have seen ourselves for what we are: flawed children of a forgiving God.

4. Waiting for the Word

The period of quiet listening, when as yet we have not received any clear knowledge of our next step, demands great patience as we "Wait for the Word." Of course, patience is required throughout our lives. Seldom do things turn out exactly as we would like them to be. Seldom do others act as we would like them to act. Life seems to be a series of "put up withs" rather than a placid enjoyment of "likes."

I believe that it is somewhat easier to "put up with" tardiness when we know what should be done, when we know that a phone call will eventually come, when we know that soon we will enter the game and need now only wait for the game to begin. It is harder to be patient when the rules of the game have not yet been given, when we are listening in "darkness" with no assurance (but hope) that the "Word" will ever come.

From personal experience I can testify to the anxiety of waiting for a publisher to phone with a decision. You listen for the phone but have no certainty that there will ever be an answer. When you know that your "great work" is to be published it is easier to sit by the phone and patiently wait for the call giving specifics about the process. Then, you at least know that the phone *will* ring sometime. There is no question that there is someone out there with the answers and that in their own good time they will tell you what is needed to get on with your life. When you listen in darkness over a long period of time, you begin to wonder if the phone will ever work, whether there will ever be someone on the other end who knows enough and cares enough to tell you what to do. It is hard to "Wait for the Word" when you have heard no word before.

I must believe that Dismas had such an experience. He spent a lifetime "waiting for the phone to ring" but only got "The Word" dying on the cross next to Jesus who was "The Word." We don't know if Dismas did anything good in his life before his last hours. But whatever happened to him before, by a grace of coincidence and conversion he was in the physical presence of the suffering Jesus as he died. He felt sympathy for the dying stranger and at last came to believe that God was near. Then, perhaps for the first time in his life, he began to hope. In those last moments of belief and hope, he must have realized that God had been with him and in him through all of his wasted years. It was not that God was absent; he had just wanted to wait to tell Dismas face to face what he needed to know. God had patience with Dismas, and Dismas must have had patience too. Through all his wandering years he seems never to have given up hope as he waited in his darkness for the gentle Word of God. So too, the Old Testament saints must have had great patience as they "Waited for the Word," looking forward to the coming of God to earth, not knowing when or how or even if it would ever happen. As Augustine remarked, because of their patient waiting they were justified by a faith in the "Word" who was yet to come: "That which we know *did* occur, they believed *would* occur" (*On Patience,* 21.18).

The same persistence in waiting for a yet unknown "Word" was demonstrated in Augustine's own life. Except for a brief bout with skepticism, he never stopped listening for the words that would give him direction. He patiently pursued Christ, the "Word," even when he was not exactly sure who

God was. He listened to the words of his mother and his friends. He read the works of the great philosophers. He heard the sermons of Ambrose and listened to stories about Christian heroes, patiently waiting for the "Word" that would tell him that *now* was the moment for his full conversion to Christ.

Such patient listening for the "Word" becomes more difficult when our listening is not peaceful, when we are subject to disaster after disaster, when we are surrounded by the curses of our enemies and the whining of those we love. Augustine believed that the classic example of this was Job in the Old Testament (*On Patience*, 12.9). It was Job's patient waiting and listening in his darkness that eventually saved him (*Sermon 398*, 10). In many ways Job was a better man than his ancestor, Adam. Both were tempted by Satan: Adam, to disobey God; Job, to blaspheme and curse God. Adam, living in a perfect world, gave into the temptation; Job, living in a terribly flawed world, rejected it. Perhaps this shows that it is sometimes harder to hear the voice of God in good times than it is in times that are bad (*Commentary on the First Epistle of John*, 4.3).

It remains a mystery why good men like Job and Augustine had to endure so much as they "waited for the Word." One obvious answer is that good people (like Job) must put up with a lot when they live in the midst of others who are not so good. The very goodness of Job probably attracted the critical attitude of his friends. His patience with his suffering also probably increased the impatience of his wife. When a person stands mute as evil swirls around him, there is the temptation to curse him for being an unfeeling "lump" or worse still, a passive fool. Job's wife was affected by the passion of the activist facing those who meekly accept their fate. She had a variant form of "road rage": an anger at seeing the one she loved lie quietly on the road of life as others rolled past and over him.

As might be expected, Augustine gave a more religious explanation for Job's troubles and, in general, to the perennial problem of bad things happening to good people. He suggested that it is a way of showing us what we are capable of:

> Sometimes we really do not know the extent of our weakness
> nor the power of our strength. Sometimes we think we can do
> more than we actually can do and then God must show us that
> we are still too weak to accomplish what we propose. Or we
> may despair of ourselves and then God must show us that we
> have the inner strength to endure. If we are in the first group,
> we must be given a lesson of humility. If we are in the second,
> we must be rescued from despair (*Sermon 208B*, 8).

Sometimes our period of "Waiting for the Word" is extended so that the experience will help us become missionaries
of hope to those still in the midst of their search. Only those
who have experienced darkness can understand others still immersed in their own darkness. As Augustine said to his
Manichean friends: "Those who condemn you do not know
how much effort is needed to discover the truth and how hard
it is to avoid error" (*Against the Fundamental Letter of Mani*,
2.2). If Augustine had not gone through his own nine years as a
Manichee, perhaps he would not have been so tolerant of those
who were still wandering. After "Waiting for the Word" over so
many years, Augustine could hope and pray that someday that
"Word" would be heard by those who were still waiting.

One thing is sure: the reason why God allows turmoil in
our lives, why he sometimes seems to be playing "hide and
seek" with us, is because of his love for us. The reason why God
allowed Dismas to wait so long for conversion, the reason why
he allowed Augustine to wander so far before finding the truth
about himself and God, the reason why he allowed Job to suffer
so much to prove his virtue, was that he loved them. So too, it
is because of his love for us and what he wants us to accomplish with our lives that he sometimes allows us to wait for a
long time before his "Word" calls us out of our darkness.

We are stronger than we think we are and God wants to
prove that to us by calling upon reserves of patience that we
never imagined we had. He wishes to teach us that we will need
such patience to accomplish our search for the God who is still
hidden. The patience demanded of us now as we "Wait for the
Word" is a preparation for what lies ahead.

3

Knowledge: The Path out of Darkness

1. Knowledge

The path out of darkness is through light. For wandering souls like me (and you?), who have been listening patiently for some direction, this light comes through a gradual "illumination" that allows us to begin to know who we are and where we are meant to go. We begin to see the truth about our "selves" and our destinies.

What must be emphasized at the very beginning is that knowledge can only be of "the truth." It must be an awareness of reality as it actually is. My knowledge captures the truth of my situation only when my judgments, my insights about the reality of my world, correspond with the fact (*On True Religion* 36.66). Error can never count as knowledge. Denial of "that which is" can only be described as "error," not knowledge (*Soliloquies*, 2.15.29). Certainly that most perfect form of knowledge, wisdom, cannot rest on an erroneous idea about what the world is truly like. If I claim to "know" that I am all-perfect, that indeed I am God, I cannot be called wise. Indeed, I am insane. Like those poor souls who laugh at a world their terrible fever has created, I am dangerously ill (*Sermon 175*, 2). No sensible person would like to be in that condition. We are made with a desire to find and face the truth, not live in fantasy.

But how can I do this? I am in direct, *immediate* contact only with myself and honest self-analysis can give me some knowledge of my *present* condition. I can know my present ecstasies and my depressions, whether I "feel good" or "feel bad."

Also, within the caverns of my mind I can discover abstract truths that seem to be eternal and immutable (the truths of mathematics and logic, for instance). Such truths are beyond doubt but they do little to reveal the ever-moving world in which I live. The truths of vectors may predict infallibly the direction of a force created by the collision of two other forces, but they tell me nothing about the direction I should take with my life today.

Although I also have direct contact with the present world beyond my "self," the perfection of my knowledge about that world must take into account the instruments through which I know. A high fever may give a distorted picture of the world I perceive. I may hear sounds and see colors that are not there. But still, with that "caveat" noted, we can agree with Augustine that it does not make sense to doubt the truth of *every* perception we have of the external world (*The Trinity*, 15.12.21). Through the wonderful power of my senses I can discover something about the environment in which I live, its sounds and smells, its colors, and its texture. Such accuracy about the *present* cannot be extended without caution to our knowledge of *past* events, even those we have experienced ourselves. Our memories are often influenced by our imaginations that sometimes make us recall the good times better and the bad times worse than they actually were. In memory, we sometimes excuse past indiscretions and magnify past triumphs.

Knowledge of past or present events that we have not experienced for ourselves is even more problematic. To know such events we must depend on the testimony of others, a testimony that may be confused by their disabilities or corrupted by their desire to deceive. But even so (as Augustine also says), it would be absurd to doubt *everything* that we learn from this source (*The Trinity*, 15.12.21). Only trustworthy elders can tell me about the past and only trustworthy prophets can tell me of a *future* that is yet to happen.

Although there are many things that I can know or figure out on my own, there is much, much more that can only be known through others. My knowledge may come through personal experience or through faith, but faith is the more powerful source in our continuing search for God. Reason can and does sometimes yield absolute certitude, but only faith can nourish hope. Not even a dedicated Cartesian will dance over the certainty of "I think, therefore I am!" but Christians have sometimes experienced ecstasy from their belief that "I am, therefore I am loved!"

If at very least I can come to realize that the still unknown God is near, ready to help in the journey that lies ahead, I am able to begin to pray (*On Christian Doctrine* 2.7.10). In my time of darkness I could not pray because there seemed to be no one there. In my time of pious listening there was a glimmer of hope, but still there was no one yet to be seen. Finally, now, the light has begun to shine. I may now begin to hope that there is a SOMEONE who has the power and the desire to help me. My knowledge is not too clear as yet. I do not know what this God *is* exactly, but I begin to reach out to him in hope.

2. The Search for God

When Augustine sat down to write his *Confessions*, he looked back over his years of wandering and summed up the odyssey of his search for God by declaring: "Late have I loved you, O Beauty ever ancient yet ever new; late have I loved you! You were inside me all the time but I was running around outside" (*Confessions*, 10.27). He had searched for happiness in many different places throughout his life. As a young boy he sought it in games. As an adolescent he sought it in being accepted. As a young man he sought it in romantic love. For a while sensual satisfaction became his god. And then it was reason. And then it was career. Finally, his god became "nonbelief." Each of these gods proved in time to be unsatisfactory. Sensuality became boring. His romantic attachment to his common-law wife came into conflict with his career. His dream of the coldly rational mind capturing wisdom was destroyed by the reality of his uncontrolled passions. Even nonbelief proved to be nonsense. All the earthly gods that he had run after so vigorously finally failed him. It was only then that (in his early thirties) he received the gift of faith and became a baptized follower of Christ.

But baptism did not mean that his search was over. He rejoiced in what he knew, but he realized that his knowledge of God would always be incomplete in this life. He reveled in his continuing thirst for God, but he knew that such desire could fade at any moment. He knew that there was still a chance of messing up his life. He was prudently fearful of his own ability to shut the doors of his life on God, just as once before he had held the doors tightly closed against him. Having found God, he did not cease his prayer "Let me know myself; let me know you!" (*Soliloquies*, 2.1.1). He knew that at any moment he could again fall into darkness, not because the Divine Light had ceased to shine, but because he had closed his eyes.

There are many lessons that can be learned from his lifelong search for the vision of God. The first is that we must be *free to believe*, free of the earthy interests that, if they come to dominate our days, will rob us of the time and energy necessary for listening to the Lord. This does not mean that we must run away from this world. Even if it were possible, it would be eminently foolish since God cannot be found except in the place where we are. We don't know where his house is. We can only wait for him to come to ours, and our house now is here in the midst of the hills and valleys of this world. We need not deny this world in which we live, but neither can we allow it to consume us, to trap us in our here and now. If it does, our lives become knotted. Going this way and that, trying to rush off in all directions at once, we become like a thread twisted back upon itself as it responds to the eccentric thrusts of its directing needle. We are knotted in place, entangled in the fabric of our present lives. We can move no further and we begin to turn over and over again in our tangled darkness (*Confessions*, 3.11).

The second fact about our search for God is that in this life it will be *never-ending*. There is no moment in our lives when we can say: "The Lord has come! I have found him finally and forever!" While we live there is always the chance of losing our God, of walking away and closing our lives to him. Even if this does not happen, we are constantly changing. We go through different stages in our lives, and the Lord needs to come in different ways with different messages. Life must be a continuing "turning towards" the Lord and a faith that does not grow will perish.

Each day the Lord has something new to say to me because each day is new. When I was young, the Lord came with encouragement to try new things. When I grew older and tasted success, the Lord told me not to take myself too seriously. When I fell in love, the Lord encouraged me to develop an innocent love, neither hurting my love nor myself. When I was sick, I needed the Lord to tell me how to bear my illness. Now that I am old, I need the Lord to tell me how to live with diminished powers. At the moment of death, I will need the Lord most of all.

The third fact about our search for God is that *we need some quiet* to pursue the search successfully. More often than not God will speak to us in the same way as he spoke to Elijah as described in the Old Testament story (1 Kgs 19:11-13). God's presence is more like a gentle breeze than a hurricane, and it occurs deep inside each one of us. If there is too much noise in our lives, we cannot hear his words.

A fourth fact about our search for God is that it will very often be *stormy*. The New Testament tells of two storms that Jesus and his disciples lived through. In the first storm (Luke 8:22-25), Jesus was in the boat with the disciples. He was close to his friends but this neither stopped the storm nor prevented them from being scared half to death. In the second storm (Matt 14:22-33), Jesus was on the shore and the disciples were already out at sea. The storm came up and this time Jesus came to his frightened disciples by walking through the turbulent waves to the stormy place where they were.

The lessons of the stories are clear. Being a follower of Christ is no protection against storms, and the confusion that we sometimes experience in life is not a sign that the Lord is far away. He may be in our "boat" already, but our pain and terror make it difficult to hear his reassuring voice. It is indeed hard to see the Lord when the skies grow dark, but he is there nonetheless, listening to our prayers. Sometimes we don't think he answers because the storm continues. Only later do we realize that storms are conquered more by living through them than by doing away with them. If we listen carefully in the midst of our storms, we may hear the same words that Jesus spoke to his frightened disciples: "Get hold of yourselves! It is I. Do not be afraid!" (Matt 14:27).

One thing is certain: we do not need to travel to some foreign land to find God. If we wait patiently, God will come to us and speak to us in the midst of our ordinary days. Of course, we must prepare for that visit by first cleansing our eyes and spirits of anything that can dull our vision, freeing ourselves from the tentacles of our times that may hold us down. But once that is done all we need do is to wait patiently in that place in life that God's providence has prepared for us. We are nailed in place, and sometimes that place is a cross. Nailed to that special cross that is our life, we cannot run to the Lord. All we can do is wait for him and turn our head in his direction.

Thus, the final (and most important) fact about our search for God is that it must begin by *paying attention* to God, just as Dismas, nailed to his cross, turned his head and paid attention to Jesus-God impaled on the cross next to him. If we pay attention to God especially by reading the story of his words and deeds recorded in Sacred Scripture, we will come to know his promise that our search for him will be successful if we do not give up, if we want to find him, if we hope to find him, if we allow him to find us.

3. The Need for Faith

It would be wonderful if we could now "see" God with an overpowering face to face encounter that would *convince* us beyond doubt of his existence. Unfortunately this does not happen in this life. This is not the land of that vision that is called "beatific." We may get a hint of God's presence from the so-called arguments of reason, but to really *discover* God, to know intimate details about God and his relationship to us, we must have faith, a faith that demands a leap into the darkness of the unknown. When in this life we speak of God, we are speaking about someone whom we have not yet experienced. We do not have direct experience of the God proclaimed by others; our direct experience is only of the "proclaimers," people who (like ourselves) are wrapped in mystery. It is for this reason that we are not forced to believe; we must choose to believe. This is the reason why Augustine defines faith as "thinking with *assent*" (*Predestination of the Saints*, 2.5).

Faith is first of all a "thinking." It is not an ecstatic movement of the emotions, a good feeling for no good reason. Faith is an exercise of the mind, a judgment that "this indeed is so." Faith goes beyond the evidence of reason but it must still "be reasonable." What it proclaims may be unlikely, but it is cannot be impossible. I must be able to "understand" in order to "believe" (*Letter 102*, 38). However, just as reason in its power to understand is the foundation for faith, faith has as its goal an *understanding* of the truth believed. When we make an act of faith in God, we do not yet see God but we at least believe that God exists. When we "know" something to be true through faith but do not yet "understand" it, then because of our natural inquisitiveness we are motivated to try to understand it (*Letter 120*, 2.8). Thus, while I "understand" so that I might come to "believe," the goal of belief is to come to "understand," to finally comprehend the truth believed (*Letter 120*, 1.3).

This is shown even by our ordinary experience. Day after day belief opens the door to great vistas of knowledge that we only later come to understand. None of us would have survived our early years without the trust we had in the friendly giants who were constantly telling us what was and was not good for us. Again, when someone says "I love you," we can never know for certain that they do. To know that we are loved is a belief rather than a directly perceived truth. Our supposed lover may indeed show us signs of affection, may indeed "act as though" they love us, but we can never see what is going on inside them. Love is an act of the spirit and their spirit is forever hidden from us. For one who is by nature suspicious, it is very easy to choose to disbelieve any proclamations of affection from others, especially when you do not consider yourself worthy of love. This is not the case with matters of direct experience. We may not think ourselves worthy of seeing the sun, but we are blinded none the less on a bright, sunny day.

When it comes to more sublime matters, matters that pertain to eternal happiness, the priority of faith is even more evident. As a "cracked Christian" I cannot know much about God except by believing. But once I come to believe the mysteries of faith as proclaimed by Christ and the Christian community, I can then go on to try to understand what these mysteries are telling me about how I should live day by day. It is not always easy to accept the hard truth revealed. This is why I must *choose* to believe. I must choose to pay attention, choose to try to understand the revelation, choose to trust that the one who reveals the truth knows what they are talking about and is not trying to deceive me.

Despite the disruption in our comfortable life that our faith can sometimes cause, there are good reasons for leaving ourselves open to belief. Considering the alternatives of living a faith-enlarged life or a life limited to what we can be absolutely sure of, it seems impractical (if not unreasonable) to choose the latter course. We simply must believe in *something* to get through life. To those who cry "I will not accept anything on faith; faith is unreasonable," Augustine responds, "Look at your daily life. What truths do you in fact experience directly? If these alone will count as true knowledge, then indeed there will be very few things that we can be said to know" (*The Trinity*, 15.12.21).

If faith is so necessary to know truths about our ordinary life, it is not surprising that it should be needed to know and accept the extraordinary truths preached by Christianity. To understand our place in the universe and get a clear idea of what God is like and what he demands of us, we need the ability to accept truths revealed by reliable witnesses. Considering what we are called upon to believe as Christians and the imperfection of the Christian community that proclaims it, it is no wonder that faith in the supernatural is a fragile gift. In some mysterious way (by the grace of God) we are called upon to believe the unthinkable proclaimed by the improbable.

When Augustine finally came to know Jesus Christ, he was not disturbed by his inability to see the face of God through what has come to be known as the "Beatific Vision." His faith brought with it the conviction that God was both outside and inside his "self." He did not yet understand that presence, but he believed in it. Like the faithful on Calvary, he was able to look at the crucified *man* Jesus and see *God.* Thereafter it was this faith that allowed him to survive the times ahead as a baptized Christian when all he could see was the darkness of his life and all he could hear was the silence of God. For Augustine it was his coming to know the person of Jesus Christ that finally allowed him to move beyond his times of darkness and patient listening. He now began to hear words telling him "What God was *like.*"

4. The Discovery of Jesus

Augustine's search for something to believe in finally came to an end when through a miracle of grace he came to believe that a man who had lived four hundred years before was in fact God himself. With that belief his persistent questions: "Who am I? What is God like? What is this world like?" began to be answered. Augustine moved out of the darkness of his previous thirty years through his discovery of Jesus, not simply the human Jesus but Jesus-God. Even though he had known of Christ the man from his early years, the discovery that this person was indeed God was a long and laborious journey. Augustine did have the advantage of being born into an environment where Christianity was flourishing in one form or another. Jesus was "known" even by the numerous pagan and mystical religions current in the North Africa of his youth. He also had the advantage of having a tolerant pagan father who did not stand in the way as his fervently Christian mother told him stories of the man Jesus who had lived so long before.

In his middle twenties (after a brief period of believing in nothing), Augustine's interest in Jesus the "man" reawakened but he still did not comprehend that this *man* could be *God* (*Confessions,* 7.19.25). He had come to revere the man Christ, but as yet he could not believe in the Christ who was divine. As he would later emphasize, again and again, such faith came to him only as an unmerited gift from God. There is no question that this belief in the Incarnation was for him an extraordinary belief, one that opened up avenues of discovery that before he could not have even imagined.

When Augustine finally came to believe in the divinity of Christ, his inquisitive nature prompted him to ask why God would want to live the life and die the death of an ordinary human being. As his knowledge of his new-found faith grew, he began to understand that the primary reason for the Incarnation was so that the human race might be redeemed. Through the suffering and death of the God-Man Jesus, the gates of heaven were opened, giving every human being the chance, not only to have a happy human life, but even to share in the happiness of God. God became a human being so that humans might have the chance to become like gods (*Sermon 192,* 1). Christ shared our human life for thirty-three years on earth so that we could share his life in heaven forever.

Of course, humanity could have been redeemed in an infinite number of ways without God taking the extraordinary step of actually becoming human. Why was this particular method of redemption chosen? Augustine suggests that perhaps God wanted not only to be *believed in*; he wanted to be *seen* (*Sermon 225,* 3). God wanted to be in some way visible to human beings so that humans might be able, not only to listen to the words of the God-Man, but to actually *see* him and come to know that the person they thought was only a good man was in fact the Good God. Those who walked with Christ did not see his divine nature (such a vision would have destroyed them) but, realizing finally that Jesus was in fact God Almighty, they could experience how God acted towards humans and then pass on that memory to future generations.

It is indeed a grand memory. The history of Jesus Christ reveals a God who cures the sick, rages against the unrepentant wicked, embraces the poor, and forgives sinners. Through the dramatic event of God becoming human and talking and walking and listening to humans, God demonstrated (and not simply declared) how much he *valued* humanity and indeed, how much he *loved* each and every human being (*The Trinity*, 13.10.13). By becoming a human being Jesus-God became the perfect *mediator* between God and humanity (*Enchiridion*, 28.108). No longer could human beings despair because of the immense distance between themselves and their God. Their God in the person of Jesus Christ had become one of them (*Sermon 313E*, 1). Through his death and resurrection he gave every human being the hope that they too could survive death (*Sermon 242A*, 1).

Moreover, through his Incarnation in the person of Jesus Christ, God not only gave *knowledge* of "What God was like." He also gave the *way* to union with God. He did this by providing the divine help (the grace) which helps us to keep on the right path and to recover when inevitably we fail. He also gave instructions on how we should act. He said: "Love God above all; love other humans as yourself!" and then gave an example of what such a life of love should look like. By living our human life he gave us an *example* of how to live on earth so that eventually we might reach heaven.

Jesus exemplified the life we should live in many ways. First, he lived a life of *detachment* from this earth. A poor man from the beginning of his life, in his last three years he became truly "homeless," wandering the roads of Israel depending on the kindness of others to supply the bread and bed he needed each night. He was the paradigm of the "pilgrim nation" that was and is the human race. He made little of earthly things by turning his back on many of the goods that we humans spend our days living and dying for.

Christ's life was also an example of the *charity* that should rule our lives. He showed that it is no good to be "detached" from things if you turn away from others. It is useless to give up "things" if you are not prepared to echo Christ's words to the Father in the Garden of Gethsemane, "Thy will be done." It is useless to give up "things" only to deny love to other human beings. Such solitary detachment can lead to pride. Rather than freeing us to look up to God, it may tempt us to look down on others whom we consider less virtuous than we are.

It is for this reason that the third lesson Christ's life teaches is a lesson in *humility*. It is certainly true that the core of his instruction on how to live was centered around a charity for others resting on a detachment from things, but his life also showed that these great good qualities must rest on a healthy humility. This is true even in ordinary everyday life. In order to love and respect others, we must first appreciate their value. When that appreciation is lacking, all sorts of crimes against love result. We "bully" others because in some way we consider ourselves to be better than they are. We are prejudiced against individuals and classes of human beings because we have come to believe that somehow or other we are more "human" than they are.

Augustine's discovery that Jesus was not only a human being to be revered but a God to be worshipped did not give him the *vision* of God he so desperately sought, but it was the source of the hope that gave him strength through the rest of his long life. He still became depressed when he saw the state of the world in which he lived. He still suffered exhaustion from his day after day labors as teacher and mentor and judge. But despite the ongoing turmoil in his life, he was able to joyfully tell his friends:

We are on our way to see the Christ who is God, and the Christ who shares our humanity is the way through which we go. We are going to him and we are going through him. Why then should any of us fear becoming lost? (*Sermon 123*, 1, 3).

Through his passionate search for the answers to life, Augustine discovered Jesus-God and through that discovery he discovered hope.

5. The Discovery of "What God Is Like"

Augustine did not gain the *vision* of God through believing in the divinity of Jesus Christ, but by reading and reflecting on the story of Christ (the life he lived and the stories he told) he did gain comforting knowledge about what God was *like*. What he discovered helped him to yearn for God more passionately and trust him more fervently. Two stories that had a special impact on him were the stories of the Good Samaritan and the Prodigal Son.

In the story of the Good Samaritan (Luke 10:30-37), God is portrayed as a wandering citizen of Samaria who saved a stranger (a Judean and thus a supposed enemy) from certain death. The good samaritan in the story represents Jesus himself, the Incarnate Son of God who lifted wounded human beings out of the abyss of their sins and treated their wounds with the healing "oil and wine" of his grace (*Commentary on the Gospel of John*, 41.13.2). Jesus, like the samaritan, carried wounded humanity on his own back (*Sermon 119*, 7) to an inn for travelers. Once there he paid for their care with his own flesh and blood, promising that someday he would come back to take them the rest of the way home.

The meaning of the story for us is that we are still in this place of healing. We are cracked and weak. We don't always know where we are going or what we are to do. Still, there is no reason for despair. We have been saved from the pit of eternal death, and someday we shall be just fine as long as we realize that we are not "cured" and continue to take the medicine that has been provided for us. Certainly we have no reason to be proud. We may have been saved but we are not yet healed. As Augustine says: "We should gladly accept being cured at this Inn. We must not boast of our health while we are still feeble. If we do that, we will never be healed because we will be too proud to take the cure" (*Sermon 131*, 6).

The story of the Prodigal Son (Luke 15: 11-32) goes even further in describing God's intimate and loving relationship to the human race. In this story God is not simply a kind foreigner who rescues humans from the pit; he is a father and we are his children. He is both our father and mother (*Commentary on Psalm 26*, 18), nourishing and protecting us so that we might be healthy and happy (*A Literal Commentary on Genesis*, 8.10.23). The story also tells us humbling facts about how children sometimes treat their parents. Augustine had no trouble identifying himself with the younger son in the story (*Questions on the Gospels*, 2.33). Like the prodigal, Augustine had taken the gifts that his father had given him (his life, his body, his mind) and wasted them in a search for earthly love and fame and good times. Just as the young son in the story left his father to find freedom in foreign lands, so Augustine fled from the call of the heavenly father to enjoy the fleshpots of Carthage and the sophisticated culture of the imperial court at Milan. Again, like the prodigal in the story, Augustine did not think of returning to God until he had nowhere else to go.

The Prodigal Son returned to his father when he was empty, when he had no one else to go to. His saving grace was that he went with humility. He had wasted his gifts. He was certainly wrong. But when he turned back to his father, he at least made no excuses. He said simply: "Father, I have sinned. I no longer deserve to be called your son." The response of the father was dramatic: "While he was still a long way off, his father caught sight of him and was deeply moved. He ran out to meet him, threw his arms around his neck, and kissed him." And when the son cried out: "I no longer deserve to be your son!" the father did not try to argue the point. He ignored it and instructed the servants: "Take the fatted calf and kill it! Let us eat and celebrate because this *son of mine* was dead and has come back to life. He was lost and is found!" (Luke 15: 20-24).

There are important lessons about God to be learned from the story. The first lesson is that God is a father who will forgive us if we ask for forgiveness, but he will not force us to return. He will help us to choose to return (perhaps by providentially allowing us to exhaust other possibilities) and then will rush forward to meet us. There may be punishment for our sins when we return (because God is a God of justice as well as kindness) but the punishment will not be forever.

The second lesson of the story is that we can separate ourselves from the Father by going to foreign places or by staying right at home. Augustine uses the older son as a symbol of all those who consider themselves to be God's chosen ones and who resent God's blessings on anyone less virtuous than themselves. The angry words of the older son tell us much about his true feelings towards the father. When he learned that his younger brother had returned home and that a party was in progress, he was furious. He would not go into the party, and so the father came out (a sign that our God will put up with our sulking at home as well as our skulking abroad). He asked his older son to please come in, but he would hear none of it. I can imagine him screaming at his father:

> For years now I have slaved for you! I never disobeyed one of your orders, yet you never gave ME so much as a kid goat to celebrate with MY friends! But when this son of YOURS returns after having gone through your property with loose women, you kill the fatted calf for HIM!

The father killed the fatted calf for his younger son and got the older son's "goat."

The story of the Prodigal Son ends there. We never learn what happened to either boy. But I suspect that if one of them ended up in hell, it was the older son. He hated his father. He resented his father giving any of his goods to the Prodigal Son because he wanted it all. He wanted all of the inheritance. Indeed, he wanted his father dead so that he could be the only god in town. Far from ever asking his father's forgiveness, the older son thought that he was owed by the father and that in being kind to the prodigal the father had sinned against HIM! The older son stayed at home. He did everything that his father asked him to do. But one thing he did not do: he did not love his father. He would not admit that all that he had was from the father. He made himself into a human god, and, if he stayed that way, he just *had* to go to hell. Heaven has room for only one God and that God is the Father.

What, then, is God like? He is so far above us that we cannot comprehend him, and yet we do know that he has reached down and saved us. More, we know that he is our Father and that the care he has for us is like the care the father had for his prodigal son. We don't know what happened to the two boys. Maybe the younger son went away again once the party was over. Maybe the older son went away too, disgusted with the father's forgiving ways. But one thing we DO know about the father in the story and our Father in heaven: he will always be ready to take back any of his children who return asking forgiveness. No matter how often we wander from our Father, no matter how far we have wandered, no matter how long we have been separated from him, we who are his children can always say to him "I'm sorry" and hear the wonderful words of the father to his prodigal son: "Let the party begin! My child has come back to me!"

Such stories about what God is like are truly heartening but they do not give us the *vision* of God that is the object of our search. Our pilgrimage towards such vision must continue. We have not yet arrived.

4

Fortitude

1. The Need for Courage

Knowing who we are and what God is like can be a thrilling experience, but it can also be frightening. It can cause us to anguish over how far we are from the vision of God we seek and make us despair of ever getting there. Such knowledge must quickly be combined with courage lest we stop dead in our tracks in our effort to "find God" (*On Christian Doctrine*, 2.7.10). We need the "intestinal fortitude" to do what needs to be done to make progress. The first step is in many ways the most difficult of all. We must *disentangle ourselves from the mundane*, from the earthly pleasures and ambitions that so often come to dominate our lives. Augustine confessed that in the last days before his conversion it was not easy for him to take the final step. He writes:

> My earthly desires tugged at me and whispered, "Will you now dismiss us after so many years?" I was held back by my old sensual hungers, fighting against giving them up so that I might be free to leap across that great chasm to the heavenly land where you, O God, dwell (*Confessions*, 8.11.26).

Augustine's problem in changing his life is not uncommon. Once we become accustomed to earthly pleasure and earthly success, it is hard to hear the call to a life driven by "other-worldly" desires. It takes great bravery to choose an unknown way of living, to give up the mundane for the sake of a promised world that we have yet to experience. But it must be

49

done. Though the affairs of this world need not be rejected completely, they must be put in their place, and their proper place is not to be the end-all and be-all of our existence. But as Augustine observes, it is not easy ". . . to deliver oneself from the deadly delight of the transient" (*On Christian Doctrine*, 2.7.10). The reason is simple: "Whenever you have possessed something with delight for a long time, it normally cannot be abandoned without great pain" (*Commentary on the Sermon on the Mount*, 1.3.10).

Only when we are free from the addiction to earthly things can we bravely *turn our love to the eternal God*. Then we dare to give our love to a person whom we have never seen. But it is hard to become ecstatic over someone who is still hidden from us. It is like trying to be passionate about a lover we have never met. We may be convinced that the "great love of our life" is out there somewhere, but it is unlikely that we will change our lives until we actually experience them. It takes great faith and hope to love the unknown but that is precisely what we are asked to do in this early stage of our search. The overpowering *vision* of the God who IS loveliness itself is still far, far away.

This "*turning to love of the eternal*" does not usually result in a mystical vision of God nor does it automatically cause us to dedicate ourselves to contemplation and lives of virtue. Perhaps our "turning" begins only with a thirst for more justice in the world. In the previous stage of knowledge, we began to realize that there is an ideal world in heaven and that there could be such a world on earth, a world dominated not simply by justice but even by love. We discover that the reality is quite different, that justice does not always triumph on earth, that very often (as Augustine sadly observes) ". . . generally the acquitted are no better than the condemned" (*Commentary on Psalm 9*, 9). Seeing the injustice around us and in us, we begin to desire something better.

Coming to see the example and knowing the teaching of Jesus, we now understand what a "better world" should look like, and we courageously begin to try to bring it about. In our search for that *vocation* that will make our best contribution to this world and eventually lead us to the wisdom and the vision of God, we again find that we must be brave. We need the bravery *to look honestly at ourselves* and identify our true strengths and true weaknesses. To some extent the abilities we have can point to the way of life we should choose. We can overcome some of our deficiencies, but some seem to be part of our nature. Thus, some mechanics would be at a loss in the world of academe and some scholars would make dangerous mechanics. Some seem perfectly suited to a life of intimate marital union; others would make even an understanding spouse totally miserable.

In our search for our vocation, we also need the bravery to admit that we are in the *wrong sort of life* and then the further bravery to *not persevere* in it. It is difficult to make such a radical decision without divine help. For many years the young Augustine knew that he had to change his life, but the habits of the past held him back. It was only because God finally gave him the grace of conversion that he was able to turn his back on his desire for earthly success and earthly pleasure (*Confessions* 8.12.30).

Finally, we need the bravery to *persevere in a life which is probably the right one* but is beginning to be a burden. We may be suddenly overcome by a feeling that our lives have been wasted, that we have been spinning wheels in cars mired in mud. We say to ourselves: "There must be something better in life than this! There must be another way of life that is easier, more fruitful, more meaningful, more important in the eyes of God and the world." We do not understand that if we have lived a particular vocation for a long time without disaster, it is most likely the place where we are meant to be. The tasks we now find so boring or frustrating are probably the best "fit" for our mediocre abilities.

This challenge to accept the life that has been given us calls for the greatest courage. This is especially so for the sick or disabled or the very old. One of the burdens of great age is to realize that all of the grand tasks of your life are behind you. You may find yourself with "nothing to do" and realize that this will not change. At least when you were young with "nothing to do," you could look forward to a time when there would be great deeds to be done. But once you are very disabled or very sick or very old, the prospect of such bright change in the future is a dream. What you *are* is what you *will be,* and all you can do is to have the courage to accept that fact and make the best of what you have. You thereby do your last great work: showing how a person can bear the limits of their life patiently and with continuing concern and love for others.

Certainly our journey towards heaven will not always be easy. As long as our earthly life lasts, the wisdom that we seek, the vision and love of the hidden God, will continue to be mostly hidden in the mist of our daily interests. Even when God is momentarily glimpsed, the intense spiritual life required for progress will be difficult to maintain. It is for this reason that in this stage of our pilgrimage we need to turn to prayer. Such prayer can be a truly brave venture in the continuing darkness of our lives, but in the very act there may arise a growing belief that there is an infinite "Someone" out there, and a growing hope that this hidden God will hear the prayer and reveal himself at least a little bit more. In that prayer the continuing struggle to find our way and purify our life becomes a bit less burdensome, and indeed sometimes carries with it its own sort of delight (*Letter 171*).

2. Brave Prayer

Soon after his conversion Augustine prayed:

O God, everything good comes to me from you and you stand ready to protect me in my times of trouble. I therefore offer you this prayer. First of all, I ask for the power to pray. If you ever left me I would just be lost, but I know that you are too good to let that happen. You are too good to allow anyone to be lost

who is really trying to find you. You would work it out some-
way that they would find you. Indeed, you are so good that I
know that you will give me the power to *try* and find you. Keep
me from making the mistake of attaching myself to anything
except you. Wash me free of all my silly earthy desires so that I
may be clear-eyed enough to see you (*Soliloquies*, 1.6).

It is not surprising that, at the beginning of his search for
the vision of God, Augustine would offer such a prayer. We
must do the same thing. So far we have reflected only on what
was happening *inside* us: our darkness, our listening, our growing knowledge, our need to be brave. The time has come to
turn our attention to what is beyond us. Through our growing
knowledge of ourselves, we begin to see that we need to be supported from outside to deal with the disorder in the world
around us and in us. Coming to know the flawed reality of life,
we turn to prayer. It is truly a *brave* prayer because it is a prayer
to a God who is still unseen. We need the strength to be able to
bravely pray and hope even when we are crushed by tragedy:
when a child dies, when a loved one leaves, when fired from a
job, when finally facing the "aloneness" of solitary old age. All
such crushing blows impel us to reach out for someone to hold
us tightly and carry us into our unknown future.

It is a good thing that prayer does not depend on always
"feeling good." Our most fervent prayers are sometimes offered
when we feel bad. It is also good that effective prayer does not
depend on fine words. Often in the midst of our distress we are
mute in body and spirit. Of course, we may pray at times of ecstasy too (infrequent as they may be), and sometimes we may
pray with bravado, but that does not make our prayers good
prayers. It is our *desire* for God, perhaps for a God who seems
distant and hidden, that makes our prayers good. As Augustine
remarked: "The desire of your heart is *itself* your prayer. Whatever else you happen to be doing, if your desire is for the heavenly rest promised by God, your prayer will continue as long as
the desire lasts" (*Commentary on Psalm 37*, 13-14).

This *desire* to pray is crucial. If we pray with many words but no desire, we are mute as far as God is concerned (*Commentary on Psalm 86*, 1). As our mouths are to the ears of those around us, so are our hearts to the ears of God. Indeed, many are heard through their silence while others are ignored despite their loud chatter (*Commentary on Psalm 119*, 9). The reason is simple: "God has greater regard for how you live than how you sound" (*Commentary on Psalm 146*, 2). However, we cannot desire God unless we *pay attention* to him and this begins with our prayer: the prayer of our voices, the prayer of our hearts, the prayer of our lives.

This is not always easy to do. We are still creatures of earth. We are like thistledown in high mountain meadows, straining this way and that, desperately seeking the freedom to fly to the peaks but held firmly in place by our earthy roots. As human beings we have a natural gravity that draws us to this world, and this weight upon our spirits has been increased by the weakness from our wounds. It is hard enough to fly when gravity pulls you down; it becomes almost impossible with weakened wings. In the midst of such difficulties it is consoling to know that God does not expect us to be *perfect* in prayer, only that we try our best. My best may be none-too-good here and now, but it is good enough if truly it is my best. Just now I may not be able to think about God without distraction. Just now I may not be able to speak to him with words that are really felt. When my loved one dies, I may piously say, "Your will be done, God!" but inside I feel cheated that my beloved has been taken from me.

Some of our difficulty in prayer comes from our inability to sense God's presence in our lives. It is true that some of the great mystics prayed through their "Dark Night of the Soul" when God seemed absent, but they were at the climax of their spiritual journey. For most of us poor clods just beginning our journey towards God, a sudden dose of "God's absence" might do us in. We would be tempted to sit down in the middle of the road and go no further, or perhaps begin running back to our remembered earthy pleasures.

A fact of life is that we can't talk to a stone wall for very long without getting bored or going berserk. If we have even a *minimal* awareness of the presence of another, we can keep up a conversation even though it seems one-sided. I have known people who were able to speak lovingly to a comatose loved one for years and years. There was never much of a response, but at least they could see their beloved there before them. They knew that they were in the living presence of a *someone*. So too, we can try to speak to God if we are aware that SOME-ONE is there, if we have at least the beginning of awareness of God's presence in our lives.

Unfortunately there are no guidelines for experiencing that Divine Presence. There is no sacred place where God waits to introduce himself to us. Indeed, our faith tells us that God is where *we* are. The divine is present in *us*. *This* place where I am now is the place of God. Why then am I not aware of this presence? Perhaps I expect too much from it. We delude ourselves, thinking that this or that is a sure sign of God's presence, and when it is not present we sadly conclude that God must be someplace else. The experiences of those saints who have gone before us teach that the Divine Presence does not always make us ecstatic. It does not always make us feel any better. Dismas felt the pain of crucifixion even though Jesus was at his side. The disciples caught in the storm were still frightened half to death even though their God was in their boat. The form that the awareness of God will take varies from individual to individual. Sometimes it may be accompanied by an emotional high; sometimes there is no emotion at all. Sometimes it will come in a moment of quiet contentment, sometimes in the patient endurance of a painful situation, sometimes in the realization that wounds can be healed.

We need the support of grace to become aware of God and begin to pray to him. To prepare for this grace we need to *eliminate our selfishness*. The reason is obvious. If all or most of our energy is directed towards ourselves, there is nothing left to direct to God. We cannot excuse ourselves by saying, "I am not thinking about myself. I am thinking about my neighbor." Service of others (in itself a virtuous endeavor) may be veiled selfishness. It is easier sometimes to pay attention to our neighbor than to our God. The return of love from those we help is very satisfying. It can make us feel very good about what we are doing. Trying to pay attention to God does not usually bring such instant satisfaction. Praying to God is sometimes boring. I have never fallen asleep teaching class. I cannot say the same about my attempts at meditation.

If we have eliminated selfishness from our lives, then we can only *wait* quietly for God to come. To do this we must reserve for ourselves some time for solitude and silence. To think about God deeply and without interruption, we must be by ourselves and inside ourselves. Most of us need physical solitude for this. Sometimes in the midst of common prayer with others we may achieve a solitary communion with God, but I suspect that such moments of common solitariness (if you will, "group solitude") are few and far between. When we are in the presence of others, we tend to think about their foibles more than God's friendship.

If only we could free ourselves of our selfishness that makes us think only of ourselves and the desirable things of this world, if only we could build for ourselves times of solitary silence in the midst of our busy days, if only we could find places of solitude deep inside ourselves to pay attention to God, then we would be prepared to receive the grace to make a brave prayer in the midst of our present troubles. Even without saying too much, our attention would gradually become fixed on God. Sooner or later, if we are patient (and sometimes great patience is necessary), God will come and we will perceive him in our cloudy life and begin to desire him. We will fulfill Augustine's prediction, ". . . our love will become our weight" (*Confessions*, 13.9), now drawing us forward, irresistibly, towards the vision of God in his heavenly city.

3. The Need for Patience

The trouble with life just now is that it does not always work out in a way that we would like. We cannot always enjoy life; sometimes we must just patiently endure it. We must at times patiently endure the circumstances of our lives, the aggravation that comes from others, the pain that comes from ourselves. Augustine was not a pessimist but a realist when he observed:

> The cataclysms of nature are not all we must put up with in this life. Much of our pain comes from ourselves or from those with whom we live. Not only must we patiently endure the evil that comes from inside us; we must also endure the evil imposed on us by others (*Commentary on Psalm 37*, 16).

Certainly there is no scarcity of internal and external conditions that must be endured in this life. Others frequently make great contributions to our purgatory on earth. This happens because all of us are "cracked" in one way or another, and from time to time we are wounded by the rough edges of those we meet. Sometimes our hurt comes from our own excessive sensitivity. Sometimes it comes from another's malice. Sometimes it comes from their ignorance.

Whatever the cause, the pain hurts just as much. The very circumstances of our lives can cause us distress. Perhaps we are surrounded by people who love us but who seem to be drifting away. Perhaps we find that we are trapped in a job that we do not enjoy. Perhaps we are in a job we love and see forced retirement on the horizon. Perhaps (like Augustine) we write a book (*On Beauty*) that no one wants to read. Perhaps (like Augustine) we try to teach students who do not want to learn.

Worse than all of these is the misery that comes from within ourselves (*On Patience*, 8.8-10.9). Physical disability is one obvious source of such agony, but a person may have an apparently ideal life with good health, good friends, fulfilling work, and at the same time be pestered by temptations to perform all sorts of degrading, embarrassing acts. Luckily we cannot be prosecuted for what we think, but no one can free us from the torment of fighting to overcome such thoughts.

With so many bad things happening inside and outside ourselves, with so many annoyances and so much anguish in life, it is no wonder that at times we are tempted to shout:

> Why is this happening? Why must I be forced to endure these things? Why do bad things happen to people who have never done anything terribly bad? If God loves me, why must I patiently endure life? Why can't I just enjoy it? If God cares about me, why do I weep so much?

Augustine responds by saying to us:

> Remember that humanity was cast out of paradise because of its reckless appetite for pleasure. Does it not seem fitting that we should be taken back only after a time of humble endurance of pain? (*On Patience*, 14.11).

In any case it does no good to complain. Impatience does not take away suffering; it only makes it worse (*On Patience*, 2.2). Having patience with an unpleasant present is the foundation for hope in a better future. The experience of Job proves this (*On Patience*, 12.9). Besides, a little discomfort in this life can have a very good effect (*Commentary on Psalm 91*, 8). At very least it prevents us from becoming too attached. As Augustine explains:

> God wants us to love only eternal life and thus he allows some unpleasantness to mix with our innocent pleasures on earth. As a result, as we move towards heaven we are not tempted to dawdle in this earthly wayside inn instead of moving on to our one and only real home (*Commentary on Psalm 40*, 5).

Of course to patiently *endure* the evils of life does not mean that we should *ignore* them. Sometimes we do precisely that. We avoid going to doctors lest we find out that we have a terrible disease (as though "doing nothing" would suddenly cure it). Knowing that we have a depraved attraction for another, we ignore the obvious solution of staying away from them. Knowing that we have an addiction to drugs and alcohol, we ignore the only sure cure given by total abstinence. Feeling anger welling up in us when we are in contact with obnoxious people, we do not face the fact that the only way to avoid "idiot rage" is to avoid idiots.

Also, to *endure* evil does not mean that we should not try to do something about it, that we are justified in remaining neutral *observers*. Sometimes this happens. For example, while we recognize the evils in our families or our churches or our society, we do not raise our voices against them. While we know of the incompetence of our leaders, we will not exert the energy to vote them out. While we see the evil that is done by a loved one to themselves and others, we piously keep silent lest we upset them. We say, "It is not MY problem," forgetting that anything that brings evil into the world becomes our problem if we can do something to eliminate it.

The most distressing aspects of life (that aspect that indeed calls for great bravery) are those times when we would like to do something about the bad things that happen to ourselves or others, but we cannot. Sooner or later we will die, and there is nothing we can do to avoid it. Our loved ones are infected with terrible illnesses that cannot be cured, only endured. We discover that our children are destroying themselves in one way or another (entering relationships that make no sense, destroying their health through their various addictions, giving up faith in God and in themselves) and, despite all our best efforts, all we can do is to stand by patiently, hoping for a miracle. History testifies that such situations are not uncommon events even in the lives of the holiest. David in the Old Testament could not overcome his son Absalom's hatred for him. Jesus could not prevent his disciple Judas from despairing (*On Patience*, 9.8).

Augustine points out that our endurance of bad times must flow from the *virtue* of patience if it is to bring us closer to life in heaven and the only motive for such a life-giving virtue is the love of God (*On Patience*, 6.5). Certainly no one would say that the endurance that criminals frequently demonstrate in pursuit of their evil plans has the same quality as the bravery of the martyrs suffering death out of love for God (*Sermon 274*, 1). We may marvel at the stamina exhibited by a robber who spends sleepless nights waiting in inclement weather to attack passing victims, but we would not consider it something to be praised. Any passion can make painful endurance tolerable but only the love of God makes it virtuous (*On Patience*, 4.3).

Patient endurance that does not come from such love for God can have a dark side. Sometimes we endure the silliness of others because we enjoy seeing them make fools of themselves. Sometimes we endure an abusive boss because we hope to get a raise through fawning, or we hope to avoid firing by groveling. Augustine's words directed towards his fifth-century readers are just as true today:

> How much risk and inconvenience do we patiently endure for the sake of wealth? How much do we put up with for the sake of empty honors? How much time do we spend waiting patiently in line to get in to see popular games and shows? All around us we see people enduring the heat of the sun, the pelting rain, the frigid cold, the bitterness and wounds of war, the beatings of their conquerors for the sake of glory, money, or sexual satisfaction. Worst of all, we live in a culture that considers such insanity perfectly sensible (*On Patience*, 3.3).

Considering the difficulty we have in putting up with the evils of life with true patience, it is no wonder that the grace of God is necessary. We need to pray always for help in developing the virtuous patience that will make our endurance a means of moving along towards the vision of God.

4. Prudent Bravery

Prudence is the virtue whereby we are able to identify and then pursue proper goals through the best means to achieve them. The fact that we need prudence as we go through life shows that human affairs can sometimes go terribly wrong. Commenting on the confusion and disruption of everyday living in his own day, Augustine asked: "Is not the virtue of prudence constantly needed to be on the lookout for what is good and what is evil?" The fact that we need prudence shows that we have evil all around us and even inside us (*City of God*, 19.4.4).

Augustine believed that Prudence was the precondition for all other moral virtues (*On the Morals of the Catholic Church*, 1.24.45). What this means is that we must be prudently temperate, brave, and just, doing what we can do to combat evil but not acting foolishly, for example,

- by starving ourselves to death out of misplaced temperance
- by trying to prove our fortitude by fighting wars that cannot be won
- by destroying ourselves trying to correct an injustice over which we have no control

Augustine speaks about two types of prudence: *prudence of the flesh* and *prudence of the spirit*. Prudence of the flesh prevents us from being reckless as we go about the task of getting through this life. Prudence of the spirit prevents us from putting all our hopes in temporal goods and from unreasonably fearing evils that afflict us here on earth (*Commentary on the Epistle to the Romans*, 49). Through prudence of the spirit we are able to see that the only important thing in life is to reach heaven and that our eternal salvation is (with help from God) the only thing that we can control (*On Free Will*, 1.13.27).

Although prudence of the spirit is obviously more important, the prudence of the flesh should not be disparaged. Being saintly is no reason for being a fool in matters of this world. With prudence of the flesh, we are able to survive this life with a certain degree of nobility. In the course of his long life, Augustine exercised such prudence on many occasions. When as a teacher he discovered that his students either did not pay attention or did not pay the requisite fee, he prudently chose to give up teaching for a career at the imperial court. He subsequently chose prudently to change his job from imperial speech-writer to Christian monk. He prudently realized that, although marriage was a great good, it was not a good vocation for him. In his life-long conflicts with those who stood in opposition to the Catholic faith, he constantly searched for the most prudent way to work for their conversion while at the same time protecting the faith of the simple folk who depended on him.

Both forms of prudence demand that we first *understand* the problem facing us and then bravely *choose* the best way to deal with it. Any course of action must be based on a realistic evaluation of the possible goods to be sought and possible evils to be avoided as well as an honest recognition of our own strengths and weaknesses. Only when we have such understanding can we intelligently take the next step and do what needs to be done and can be done to achieve the desired good or avoid the perceived evil. With knowledge in hand we can then choose intelligently the course of action to follow. If our choice is guided by prudence, we will neither be too timid nor too reckless. There is an element of truth in the old saying: "Fools rush in where angels fear to tread." It is not prudent bravery to rush in as a savior against an evil we have not understood or cannot control. It is foolishness.

We need both types of prudence in dealing with all the times of our lives: our past, our present, and our future (*83 Diverse Questions*, 31.1). We must be prudent with respect to the *past* by "letting it go." We can perhaps learn from our past mistakes, but we should not let them dominate our present. We should fight against the temptation to scrupulosity (perhaps the most damaging of psychological maladies) where we have doubts that past sins can ever be forgiven. The wounds we have caused in others and in ourselves are now scarred over. Going back to make amends again and again may only open up the wounds once more. As a general rule, trying to "relive the past" is just foolishness. Speaking from experience, for me in my eighth decade to act like I was twenty (once again rushing the net, partying all night, flirting with young maidens) would not only be foolish and pitiful. It would be downright *painful*.

Prudence in our *present* means that we do not try to confront and overcome *every* evil. It is just prudent and common sense to involve ourselves only in those situations where we have the power and reserves of strength to make a contribution. For example, it is imprudent to believe that we can always make the lives of our children somehow better. When children get to a certain age, they must be left to go their own way. All the talking in the world will not change them. They must be left (and sometimes forced) to take responsibility for their lives, hoping that a memory of their loving upbringing will eventually help them straighten out their lives. After all, the Prodigal Son came back to the father only when the money ran out and Augustine was converted to Christ only after thirty years of seeking happiness in any other way.

It is also imprudent to believe that we can still do a job that is (and perhaps always has been) beyond our capacities, struggling into work (when we don't need to) when we are long past the time when we can make a worthwhile contribution. I realized that I made a prudent decision when I retired from teaching after forty-four years and no one tried to dissuade me. Augustine showed such prudence when, as an old man of seventy-one, he retired from the active ministry, realizing that someone else could do it better.

Prudence with respect to the *future* means we should make realistic plans based on our true abilities and opportunities. It was the prudence shown by a fellow Augustinian who, when he was still young, proclaimed: "If they send me to the foreign missions, I will of course go. I will DIE, but I will go!" His honest analysis of his talents was accepted by his superiors and he was able to live a long and fruitful life serving the needs of his old neighborhood. Meanwhile the missions got along very well without him. My friend had learned the important lesson that prudence begins with an honest admission of our own limits and with a hope that God will see our "pretty good" efforts and judge that they are good enough. After all, God is a God of love, and he certainly would not expect us to "burn ourselves out" trying to do great things that are far beyond our competence.

5. The Bravery of Perseverance

Augustine once said that the fundamental task for us in this life is twofold: we must *control ourselves* and we must *endure* (*Sermon 38*, 1). We must control ourselves on the good days so that we will not be so overcome by the joy of feeling fine, the joy of feeling victorious, the joy of being in love, that we become crazy with our temporary present ecstasy and refuse to go on with our lives. Sometimes on our good days we humans do go a little insane. We pitch our little tent next to our delicious "nows" and dance and dance as though "now" would be "forever." It is on such good days that there is a need for us to control ourselves, fervently enjoying the moment but not trying to hold onto it. No matter how hard we try, we cannot stop time. We can't stay young forever. We can't hold onto our loves forever. Our times move on and so do we. We are irresistibly drawn into our future. The river of our days rolls on and we cannot stand against it without being destroyed.

We must control ourselves in the midst of our exciting days, but we must also *endure* the lengthening of those days that are not exciting, days which may become increasingly burdensome because they are filled with pain or because they just seem to be all the "same." These days filled with "sameness" are the days on which we feel sluggish in our lives and somewhat useless and very much alone. There is no question that there is a weariness that comes from any kind of prolonged living this side of death. Indeed, some of us seem to fear getting tired even of eternal life. Augustine spent much effort in reassuring his friends that if they made it to heaven they would not be bored there (*Sermon 243*, 9). They just did not seem to be too sure that eternal happiness would be all that happy. The first heavenly day might be fine but what about the next and the next and the next *ad infinitum*? Even Eden seems to have paled for the first humans, and they went off looking for something entirely different.

We are all pilgrim people, on the road to a distant place that is our true home, and there is a deep-boned tiredness that comes with days and years of traveling. A pilgrim may be exhilarated at first with the excitement of each new day's possibilities, but as the days lengthen into months and years, tedium can build. It gets to the point where you begin to think that for any society and indeed for any human being the best that can be hoped for is mediocrity. As we plod through life seeking that heaven where good is triumphant, where no one has problems, where there is universal peace, where there is no wasting time on trivialities, we may slowly run out of steam after too many days on the road.

I have heard that when wandering nomad tribes met on the roads of Afghanistan, they would greet each other with the words: "Staru Mashai!" (May you not be weary!). It is a fitting prayer for one who has been on the road for a long, long time. In the psalms this weariness of the tiring traveler was recognized in the admonition: "Trust that God will protect us from the evils that come at night and the scourge of the noon-day devil" (Ps 91:5-6). In medieval times this image of the noon-day devil was used to stand for the special temptation that can come to us after years of doing the same thing day after day. It is the temptation to flee from the weariness of accustomed roads, to strike out after something new or to just give up all effort and sit by the side of the road.

When this noon-devil attacks me, I may begin to reach for anything that promises more excitement than the loves and life that have begun to bore me. It is not that my accustomed life is so bad; it is just too filled with *sameness!* The devil whispers:

> The only thing wrong with you is the place you are, the job you are stuck with, the people who surround you. You need to seek new horizons. THEN you will be able to fly again! Why plod along your usual paths when you could reach for the stars if only you would break free from your old life?

It is a destructive temptation if I give in to it. In such foolish experimentation I could destroy myself. I would discover to my horror that the only problem with my life is ME! I would discover that in fact I am nothing more than an aging wounded beast with crazy dreams, that I am a weary creature who suddenly has become long on silliness and very short on the grace of perseverance.

This gift of perseverance is necessary for every human being to get through life, but it is especially important for those who are trying to live a "good" life, a life in imitation of Jesus Christ. Those who are identified as "good people" have the burden of the expectation that they will *always* be good, that their supposedly good character will *always* shine through in difficult times. Such a life of virtue stretching into a seemingly limitless future is indeed a very good life, but it also can be very, very boring. You get to the point where there seems to be no excitement in being good day after day. You begin to feel like the vulture in the poster once given to me when I was in college administration. The old bird was sitting on a brilliantly orange dead tree underneath a bright blue sky looking stolidly out over a shimmering yellow desert. It had obviously been sitting there for a long time, hunched over with eyes half-closed next to an equally somber friend. Finally it muttered to its neighbor: "PATIENCE, HELL! I want to KILL something!" The message of the picture was clear: old birds can get bored even in a world of brilliant hues if they sit too long on the same branch. It had an immediate effect on my career as a college administrator. I resigned. It also had a message for me as a struggling Christian. Through the grace of God I may be mostly good, but it takes another special grace to keep me from becoming good and bored.

The fact of the matter is that the longer we live the more ways perseverance will be needed. The final challenge will be to persevere in our death patiently and with anticipation for what is to come. Once we die we will not need perseverance any more; we will have persevered. But up to that point we cannot be sure that we will make it. Even when he was seventy-four years old, Augustine worried whether or not he would finally persevere. As he told his friends:

> A perseverance whereby one perseveres clinging to Christ to the very end is a very great gift of God. I say "to the end" because it

is only when life is over that the danger of failure is past (*On Perseverance*, 1).

Augustine prayed for perseverance until his dying day. He was not unhappy nor was he fearful for his future. He prayed for perseverance because he was convinced that he would die as he was born, a cracked pot, and that a last-minute failure was always possible. But he was also happy because he knew that soon his struggle would be over. He was happy because he remembered the words of his mentor, St. Paul:

> Remember that Jesus Christ, a descendant of David, was raised from the dead. . . . You can depend on this:
> If we have died with him
>   we shall also live with him;
> If we hold out to the end
>   we shall also reign with him (2 Tim 2:8-12).

The dying Augustine remembered those words and knew that soon he would realize that promise. At the moment of death, he sighed with joy because he knew only then that he had persevered.

5

Love

1. The Nature of Love

The time has come to speak of love. Up to this point in our search for God, we have concentrated on what was happening inside us: our darkness, our listening, our knowledge, our fear. Now the time has come to get out of ourselves and reach out to others and, if possible, be united to them. Augustine believed that it was only through the gift of the Holy Ghost called *Counsel* that we are able to reach out in love to other human beings (*Commentary on Psalm 12*, 2). In the previous stage of our journey, we learned that we needed the mercy of God. Now we begin to understand that if we expect to receive God's mercy, we must show mercy to other human beings, not wreaking revenge for the real or imagined "hurts" that they have done to us (*Letter 171A*). It is only through such loving compassion that we can hope to be like those "Blessed" described in the Beatitudes (*Commentary on the Sermon on the Mount*, 11.4.1).

Showing loving mercy is one way of being related to others, but (unfortunately) it is not the only way. We may *hate* them, be *indifferent* to them, love them with a *selfish love*, or love them with a pure *benevolent love*. It is only this last form of love that has the power (when returned) to unite us to a loved one in a love of friendship. A convenient way of understanding each of these relationships is to consider how they might observe the commands of the so-called "Do No Harm Principle" that

1. As far as possible we should not bring harm to others.
2. As far as possible we should rescue others from harm.

Obviously if my relationship to another is characterized by *hatred*, I not only ignore both commands; I act contrary to them. The virulence of my hatred drives me to cause as much harm to them as I can. If I were moved to rescue them from some impending harm, it would only be so that they might suffer greater harm later on. My goal is not union with them but separation. Indeed, if possible, I would seek their *annihilation*. If my attitude towards others is pure *indifference*, my goal is not to harm them but just not to be bothered by them. If I acknowledge their existence at all, my attitude is one of absolute neutrality. I am neither for them nor against them. For example, if I were indifferent to God and someone asked me how I felt, I might say: "Well, he may or may not exist, but in either case it has nothing to do with me." If I am indifferent to human beings, this does not mean that I have no interaction with them. Unless I live the life of a hermit, I must deal with others every day. However, although I am quite aware of the stream of humanity passing by in all its sizes and shapes, I could "care less" about them unless they begin to encroach on my space. Like the anonymous drivers speeding past me on the highway, others become a "problem to be addressed" only when they "crash" into my life and disrupt it. There is no interest in making them friends or loving them or continuing any connection with them once my suit for damages is concluded.

Obviously neither hatred nor indifference can bring me closer to union with others. The only force powerful enough to do this is the complex act of *love*, a decision to seek some good with the goal of becoming one with it. A wave of emotion whereby I *feel* good may be part of the attractiveness of the object, but only choice can move me towards it. Such movement depends on the preconditions of *knowledge* and *delight*. I cannot choose something I do not know and I will not wish to be united with someone who does not in some way delight me. Without knowledge of and delight in the other person I will never come to love them and, not loving them, I will not be drawn to become one with them.

The goal of love is union. To love someone means to wish to be united with them, to make them my own, to have them consume my *"own-ness."* When I fall in love with some entrancing "other," I am not content to pine for them from afar. I do not want to contemplate them; I want to rush to them and hug them with a powerful embrace, crushing their loveliness into the gap, the hunger, the thirst that their gracefulness has caused in me. Until that happens I feel incomplete. Until I become "two in one flesh" with them, I am discontent. When I am overcome with love for another it is like coming upon a pool of deliciously cool water on a hot day and wishing to jump in and be immersed in its delight.

This loving union is clearly quite different from just knowing them. It is true that when I think about my past and present loves, I am in a way united to them. They are in my mind or in my memory. I have been enriched by knowing them but my knowledge does not make me become *like* them. When I love them there is a quite different effect. My life changes. To use Augustine's image, they become stuck to me with the glue of love. They leave in me "footprints" which stay in me wheresoever I go (*Trinity*, 10.8.11). I am wherever they may be. When I love someone, there my heart begins to dwell (*Commentary on the Gospel of John*, 2.11.2).

To just know another will not make me love them; they must also *delight* me. Even if I had complete knowledge of another, it would not follow that I would necessarily fall in love with them and rush to be united with them. I must first find them delightful. Delight is what drives me to seek union with this person rather than that person. I must first see my beloved as a good which promises bliss when embraced. Over the years I have known many lovely people, but only a few have caused the ecstatic delight which drew (and still draws) my love.

The reasons for the delight that causes love are complex. We may love others with a *benevolent love* because of the good we see in them or with a *concupiscent love* because of the pleasure they give to us. This last form of love is obviously not very laudable (more appropriate to rutting buffalo than to human lovers), but it may be the beginning of something more noble. Even with concupiscent love I am at least drawn outside of myself, and this first tentative step beyond my "self" may eventually lead to a benevolent altruistic love.

Benevolent love is the highest form of love, a love whereby I seek nothing for myself but only for my beloved. This is the sort of love that the great saints expressed for God even in the midst of their "dark night of the soul," the times when, far from being overcome by the vision of God, they were not even sure he existed. Obviously such great love can only come through divine intervention. It is the love that St. Paul spoke about when he wrote: "The love of God has been poured into our hearts through the Holy Spirit who has been given to us" (Rom 5:5).

This is the perfect love that will eventually bring us to union with God. It is a "love of friendship" of the highest order. Through faith we already know that God loves us as a friend, loving us for the good he perceives in us. Our task is to try to return that pure, benevolent love by loving God because of the infinite goodness we have come to see in him. Such vision will not occur in this life, at least not as a permanent state. Our eyes are too clouded; our lives are too confused. But we can practice for loving and uniting with the infinite good that is God by loving and uniting with the reflections of that goodness that we see in other human beings. In trying to become friends with God, we can practice by trying to love each other with a truly friendly love.

2. Friendly Love

Augustine once said that to live a somewhat happy life here on earth two things are essential: good health (which he never had) and good friends (which he had in abundance). It is only through the love of friendship that we can become "one" with others and with God. To love God because of the benefit he brings us is not enough. Eventually we must come to love him because of the good that he is. So too with our human loves. We may begin loving them because of the pleasure they give us, but if our love is to be lasting and true we must love them with the love of friendship.

Friendship can only exist when it is the highest form of love, a love of *benevolence*, a love which literally wishes the other well. This does not mean that friends will always agree, but at least they must always *care* for each other, desiring that only good things will happen to the one they love. A love of friendship must be *altruistic*, valuing the good that IS my loved one rather than the good or the pleasure that they bring to me. Such love cannot be a jealous love. When I value them for what they are in themselves, I am not upset when they also love others. Indeed, perhaps the greatest sign of my friendly love is to be happy when my beloved is happy with someone else.

It is in our nature to need human friends, but to find them is a difficult task. Friendship is not created by a union of bodies; it is a "oneness of heart" (*Against the Academics*, 3.6.13). Therefore, it can and does exist over vast expanses of space and time. When those we love are the last thing we think of at night and the first thing we think of in the morning, they are never far away. We can kiss them with our spirit while we hold them in our heart. But such unity of heart cannot exist unless our love for another is *requited* (*83 Diverse Questions*, 31.3). We can love (desire) many things without any return of love, but to be a friend to another demands that they also be friends to us. Friendship cannot exist with someone who does not know us or does not care about us.

A unity of heart also demands that there be some degree of *equality* between friends. We love our friends *as* ourselves, no more or less than ourselves. The eyes of friends neither look down nor look up to their beloved; they look *at* them. Like a delicate rake caressing soft sand, the love of friendship has a leveling power, smoothing out the differences which come from our being unique individuals. We must love ourselves and our friends in the same way, not as ends in themselves but as means whereby we can together each achieve our one eternal good: God himself (*On Christian Doctrine*, 1.22.21).

On the practical level to be friend of another means that we must be willing to bear their burdens and to allow them to bear ours. In a perfect world friendship would only need to express itself in the enjoyment of the other in unending good times. In such a world we would embrace them not because they needed us but because we rejoiced in them. This indeed would be the highest form of love, a love that "wants" another, not "needs" another (*Catechizing the Uninstructed*, 1.4.7). A love offered to our friends in their good times is not tempted to subordinate them because of their need. It simply rejoices in being with them because of the good that they are. But in this life the ideal state where friends never "need" each other does not last very long. Bad things happen and it is then that friendship is tested.

As we trudge through the river valleys of this life, we are like deer struggling against the current of our times, and sometimes we are called upon to take the lead (*83 Diverse Questions*, 71.1). There comes a time in life when each of us needs a place to rest our weary heads and there is no better place than in the arms of one who truly loves us. Friends may be delightfully sunny and breezy in good times, but if they go away at the first threat of a storm, they are not true friends at all.

The problem with trying to develop a love of friendship with others (or, indeed, with God) is that we do not know them very well. Solid friendship must be based on *truth* (*Letter 155*, 1.1). It must begin with some understanding of the "reality" that is the "other." If I do not know the real "them," and they do not know the real "me," our supposed friendship will be a fragile fantasy based on fiction. It is for this reason that maintaining a real friendship with another human being will always be a difficult and demanding task. Our knowledge of them will always be imperfect. That "inner self" that is the core of their character is constantly in flux. Even if we know who they are today, their desires and their fears, their passions and their convictions tomorrow may be different. Even today that inner spiritual core that is their true person is only partially revealed to us. Every individual is like a dark chamber surrounded by thick walls and these walls can neither be pierced completely by love nor scaled successfully by words. As Augustine observed: "Within our consciousness there is a great solitude which can neither be experienced nor seen by anyone else" (*Sermon 47*, 23).

Since we cannot know what is going on inside others, friendship must be based on *trust*. Our trust must be so strong that we dare to be *frank* with each other, free to say what we like and dislike about each other, free to share passions, fears, hopes, and dreams (*83 Diverse Questions*, 31.3). It is indeed taking a chance to be so open, to trust so much, but it is worse never to trust anyone. In Augustine's view such caution, far from being prudent, is deadly (*Faith in Things That Are Not Seen*, 2.4). The difficulty in knowing another must not make us overly cautious, refusing to give our love to anyone until they prove themselves friendly to us beyond a shadow of a doubt. The paradox is that we can never be completely sure of the heart of another, but the only way to truly know another is by opening our heart to them as a friend (*83 Diverse Questions*, 71.5).

It is no surprise that the first command of the Holy Ghost's gift of "Counsel" is "*to forgive*." Since human friendship will always be a relationship between "cracked" individuals, we must expect that those we love will never live up to our expectations perfectly. Sometimes they will do the wrong thing; sometimes they will wrong us. In such situations the sign of our friendly love will be our willingness to forgive them for the past and hope for a better future.

Only in heaven will our love for each other be perfected. Only there will we truly know the glory of each other. Only there will we finally be the *best* of friends with ourselves, our loved ones, and that loving and lovely God who, in the person of Jesus Christ, walked this earth as our friendly companion.

3. The Joy of Love

Augustine once wrote the following to a distant friend:

> For a while you are hidden from me and I tell my heart to be brave but it does not pay attention. I am glad that I can't stop being happy when you are with me and can't stop crying when you are far away. Now when you are far away my only consolation is in embracing my sadness (*Letter 27*, 1).

His words express well the sometime joy and sometime heartache that comes when we are deeply in love with another human being.

His sentiments are reflected in God's great love song to the human race, the Song of Songs:

> For steadfast as death is love
> relentless as the nether world is devotion;
> its flames are a blazing fire.
> Deep waters cannot quench love,
> nor floods sweep it away.
> Were one to offer all he owns to
> purchase love,
> he would be roundly mocked (8:6-7).

The canticle reminds us of two glorious facts about our life just now: first, we are waiting for the coming of a God who loves us; second, it is possible for us to experience the bliss and wonder of true love even as we continue our somewhat laborious way through life.

If we have never felt the passion of human love, it may be difficult for us to understand God's love. John put it very simply when he wrote: "Let us love one another because love comes from God. Whoever does not love does not know God, for God is love" (1 John 4:7-8). Augustine repeated the same idea when, after trying to explain what the love of God might feel like, he cried out in exasperation: "Give me people who love! They know what I mean! People who are cold, who have never been on fire with love, will just not know what I am talking about" (*Commentary on the Gospel of John*, 26.4.3).

The great joy in loving and being loved is that when we are embraced by one who really loves us, we know it is because they really do care for US. We are cherished for what we are. Such love brings a quiet calm into our lives. Though not passionless, it need not be passionate. Though intimate, it need not have constant verbal communication. To rest in the arms of a beloved is a quiet thing, as close to becoming one with them as we can make it. The sound of their breathing becomes indistinguishable from our own. Our hearts beat in unison and our spirits join together. We face the world now not as two but as one.

In such an intimate love, though each is possessed by the other, neither is consumed. Indeed, a lover's individuality and freedom is enhanced by the expansion of spirit that the beloved causes. You cannot force your beloved to completely immerse themselves in you because you can never be more than a part of their lives. So too, you cannot give yourself totally to them because they can only be part of your life. Even if you have a lifetime romance, you can still only clutch a piece of each other's lives. This is part of the pain of being loved by and loving another human being. We always die wanting more. In this life we never taste enough love. No human being can give us all the love we want. There is only one person who can do that: God himself. He is the only one with an infinite capacity for love and an eternity to exercise it.

Sad to say, even the greatest love between humans is a fragile thing. Even a slight tug of selfishness can separate us. Hurt feelings, misunderstandings, foolish and misdirected passion, pride . . . these are the fingers that untie the knots of affection that bind us to each other. Even simple indifference causes our bonds to dry up and rot. We are left with nothing but yellowed strands of a love that once was new and strong but now is no more. To be tied to another by love needs constant care, a weaving and reweaving of joined lives. Without attention and nourishing, the connection can break and we drift apart without even realizing it. It a true tragedy when this happens. We lose someone who knew those inner parts of us that no stranger ever sees: our secret fears, our passions, our hopes, our childish confusions.

All of us have our public facades, those presentations of ourselves that others expect of us. It is not a deception because our public side is part of our person too. But it is only a part. Sometimes it is a part that is distorted by our puffing up this or that attractive aspect of ourselves which seems appropriate to the moment. Thus, there are times when we are scared to death at the very moment we play hero for our loves. At other times we play the saint for those who come to us for a prayer or an answer to the mysteries of their lives. We give no hint that deep down inside we are just as confused as they are.

If we become adept at such roles, we may even come to believe that we are indeed lovely and brave and holy. We should know better. Our dreams and fantasies should show us that we are not all sweetness and light, that we are only "cracked" human beings like all the rest. The joy of having a true love is that they will love us despite our cracks. A true love is one to whom we can reveal our secret selves without fear of being rejected. A true love is one before whom we can stand naked without fear of laughter or horror.

If we have such a true love, we can have fun with them without embarrassment. When two lovers swing arms as they stroll down city streets or chase each other merrily over a seaside meadow, on-lookers smile and say: "Well, what do you expect? They are very much in love." Indeed, our human loves allow us to play the child again. We can crawl on the floor with our baby. We can walk hand-in-hand with our fiancée. We can hold in silence that one whom we have loved for a lifetime. We are not embarrassed because eccentric behavior seems expected of those in love (*Sermon 161*, 10).

Even distant loves can brighten our lives. In my heart I live in past precious moments by holding my loves once again. In my heart I live in the future possibility of holding them forever.

When I love someone who is not here just now, I lean towards that future when we shall be together again. When I am far away from the one I love, I live each moment in that distant treasured place that holds them.

But can I truly love someone who is far away? Yes, indeed! I do so every day. Some of my loves live in distant places. Some of my loves are on the other side of death. I no longer can see my departed loves but I am still warmed by their memory. I am comforted by my dreams of them. I look forward to being with them again someday. I know that I have not lost them because the ache of their absence is part of my every "here" and every "now." As I sit by myself in my solitary room, I rejoice in the affection of those I can no longer see. Love is an act of choice, and I can choose and be chosen even though separated by space and time from my love.

We are fortunate if we have given our love to another human being because this prepares us to give ourselves in love to the Lord when he comes. Having given ourselves to others in love, having forgotten about ourselves for the sake of our human love, we open up space in ourselves for God. Our love stretches us. We reach out of ourselves to a good that is beyond ourselves. We become bigger as our spirits strain toward the good that is our beloved. Just as our hearts and minds and spirits (nurtured by memories of past times together) can continue to live in the place where our distant loves live, so too we can learn to live in a land of love that is our future, a land where we will walk forever in the embrace of our Lord.

The apostle John tells us that God is with us when we are joined to another human being in love. Augustine is even more specific when he writes: "If you begin to love you become more perfect. Have you begun to love? Then God has begun to dwell in you" (*Commentary on the First Epistle of John*, 8.12). We don't know in what guise the Lord will come to us in the future. Perhaps in the past he came dressed as he was at Cana, ready to dance with us at the good times of our lives. Perhaps he came dressed as he was when he embraced the Judean children, ready to play with us and hold us and bless us. Perhaps he came dressed as he was when he came to Martha and Mary, ready to weep with us by the grave of a human love. Perhaps he has already come to us dressed as he was on Calvary, ready to lie with us naked and alone on the cross of our lives. Perhaps he has come in an infinite number of different ways in the past, but none of these can predict how he will come the next time. But this we do know: however he comes he will come as a lover.

Augustine says that our joy in heaven will consist in our enjoyment of God and also our enjoyment of our human loves forever and ever (*City of God*, 19.13). For the first time in our lives, we will not fear to reveal ourselves to those we love (*Sermon 243*, 5). To be honest, it is hard for me to see how this can happen. Just now I fear that my earthly loves would run away if they ever saw my fantasies, my vanities, my confusions. I am not sure that my human loves could stand seeing me as I really am. I do love them dearly but I don't want to hurt them or lose them. Thus now when I say the words "I love you" I sometimes speak from hiding. I keep secret my mad passions, my doubts, my fears. I hope there is no meanness in this. It just seems realistic to admit that now we can sometimes wound each other with the truth. Just now we need secrets to protect true love. Indeed, I suspect that not a few marriages are saved by what has been left *UNsaid!*

In heaven things will be different. All of us will be filled up with those noble, pure, caring, wise thoughts that we pretend to think about each other in this life. In heaven I will finally be mellow. My loves will be able to drink of my cool, clear feelings for them and be refreshed, and perhaps then they will come to understand that even now I am loving them as best I can.

We know that God will come for us at the end of our time on earth as a lover. He has already written the love song that he will be singing. It is a song that echoes in the heart of any human being who has ever been in love:

> Arise, my beloved, my beautiful one, and come!
> See, the winter is past the rains are over and gone.

The flowers appear on the earth,
the time of pruning the vines has come,
and the song of the dove is heard in the land.
Arise, my beloved, my beautiful one, and come! (Song of Songs
    2:10-13).

4. The Pain of Love

It may seem strange to speak about the wonderful experience of love as a cause of pain but so often it is. Even the most
perfect love brings its own share of trials and tribulations. This
is an imperfect world and no matter how devoted human
lovers want to be, they are hindered by the fact that they, too,
are imperfect.

Such imperfection shows itself in a number of different
ways. When we first fall in love with some lovely "other," there
can be some nasty consequences. The young Augustine found
this out when he fell in love with the lovely lady who would become the mother of his son Adeodatus. He describes his experience in his *Confessions*:

> I fell in love and my love was returned and captured me in its
> warm embrace. My ecstasy tied me in knots with cords of tor-
> ment. I began to be pounded with the flaming whips of jeal-
> ousy, suspicion, fear, anger, and bickering (3.1.1).

Augustine was passionately in love, but it was a love that
tried to consume its beloved, to possess her completely for his
own, to deny her any other human love. He was terrified that he
would someday lose her. He became angry and irritable when
she seemed to be not completely devoted to him. Without doubt
he experienced the ecstasy of having a lover, but his imperfection
made it impossible for him to be one with her in any reasonable
way. He learned the sad lesson that he expressed years later:
"There seems to be an abundance of the wrong sort of love
around and all too little of the right sort" (*Sermon 368*, 3).

Love can be especially painful when it is not returned. That
great "love of our life" may be quite pleasant about it, but it

quickly becomes clear that they have no desire for the "intimate union of hearts" that we so desperately desire. It is even worse when the pain of love's absence comes from a love that once was but has now faded. Sometimes this happens even to the most passionate love affair. The deep affection that before bound the lovers together has now faded. When the young Augustine fell in love, he might have believed that his passion would never cool. He could not have imagined that ten years later he would send his "beloved" away for the sake of his developing career.

The fact of the matter is that sometimes love does fade. Oh it may still be a raging fire in *our* hearts, but it has obviously cooled in the heart of our beloved. The object of our affection suddenly becomes the cause of our dejection. Great love affairs are sometimes dissipated by changing places, changing times, and changing lives. Returning to visit an old love after a long absence, we are excited remembering the days when we had shared hearts, when there seemed to be not enough time to talk about all the things we wanted to talk about, when we delighted in giving and receiving gossip about the big and little events in our daily lives. We look forward to renewing the intimacy, picking up where we left off, sharing each other's life as we once did so long ago.

And so we travel to the place where they are. We let them know on their voicemail that we have arrived and patiently sit by the phone waiting for their excited response. But there are no calls. When we do run across each other by accident, we share only those polite trivialities usually reserved for passing acquaintances. In the past we seemed to share each second of each other's lives, but now we ask "What's new?" and respond "Nothing much" and go on about our business. Separateness has made us like distant ships passing in the night, signaling each other across the sea with sterile and neutral crackling sounds. They, like us, are still trying to make their way to safe harbors, but now we do so by different paths.

There can be great pain in such experience if we honestly (and foolishly) believed that indeed "absence would make the heart grow fonder." There is even greater foolishness if we try desperately to take up our old place in the lives of old loves who have moved on. Old wines are obnoxious when they become too intrusive, when they impinge too insistently on loves whose tastes have changed over the years. Better by far to shrug one's shoulders and say: "That's Life!" To pine for a former love is not unusual, but it makes no sense to agonize forever. It is better by far to let them go and concentrate on the past good times shared, giving thanks for the blessing that allowed the currents of our lives to bring us together for even a brief moment. We still look at them with affection and are happy that they have found happiness with someone else. But it still hurts. We carry the pain of remembering what once was, realizing that it will never be that way again.

Even when our love stays strong over the years, there are still occasions when it can cause great pain. For instance, there are the times when we see that things are going badly for those we love and we can do nothing about it. It is easier to be sick oneself than to watch the growing illness of someone we love. We may pretend that we are distressed only because of their growing weakness, but often there is some self-interest at the root of our panic. To be sure we are upset because our friend is not feeling well. When we truly love someone their joy becomes our joy; their pain becomes our pain. They are truly part of us, and we share their life. But we cannot share their death, and that is why we tremble. If they move on, we shall be left alone. Though we may rejoice that they are moving on to a new life without pain, we cry for ourselves because all we can see in our future is the same old painful life to be lived now without the friend who made it somewhat bearable.

Thus when our loved ones get sick we worry about what will happen to them, and we worry about what will certainly happen to us if they don't recover. From the very beginning of the illness, we taste the terrible vacuum, the gap in our lives that will be left by their death. When young lovers promise in marriage to love "till death do us part," they really don't mean it. If their love is deep and true, their love will continue when one dies and bring with it a wrenching pain of loss. This agony of absence is the dark side of that coin of love that brings such ecstasy when our beloved is with us. It may have been heaven to live with them; it certainly is hell to live without them.

There is a quite different type of pain when you see your beloved hungry or confused or overcome with sorrow, and you are unable to provide the food or direction or solace that they so desperately need. It is agony for a parent to see their grown children wandering homeless in the uncaring city, unwilling or unable to come back home. It is agony to see a loved one trapped in the frightened confusion of a crippled mind. We cry out, "Take my strength; take my health!" as we stand by and watch those we love being destroyed. We are helpless and our hearts are torn apart. All we can do is stand by and let nature take its course, being present to those we love in their illness, being tolerant of the wayward knowing that we can do little to change them beyond giving them the memory of a loving home and a door that will always open if someday they knock. All we can do is to love them and leave them to God.

It is bad enough when you are not able to help another in their time of misery, but it is even worse when you are the cause of the misery. You suddenly realize that you could have eased their hurt if only you had acted more sensibly. Sometimes we are tempted to pursue a love that is already committed to another with little consideration for the effects of such unthinking infatuation on others. God help those we love with such selfish passion! We may cause them terrible injury if we forget that the happiness of fulfilled human love involves more than just being united with the beloved. It must also include bringing good to them. Human love must begin with doing no harm.

The cruel paradox of human love is that you can always make your loved one weep. You cannot always make them smile. You can hurt your love more deeply, unintentionally than the intended malice of an enemy can. You can injure your love more terribly than any stranger can. This is so because love tears down all defenses. It leaves you naked and exposed to the least soothing caress and to the worst wounding blow. Love wounds may be unintentional, but this does not prevent them from being deep and piercing with jagged edges. So tender are such wounds that it is sometimes impossible to make amends without inflicting new pain. You try to heal your love's anguish only to withdraw with tear-filled haste when you realize that you are only increasing the damage.

We must be prepared to let go of every human love if it seems to be the right thing to do. Sometimes our love for another is proven by our willingness to separate. Such separations may be painful, but with the grace of God we can get through them. We humans are as changeable as a sandy beach. The holes left in our lives by loves who have gone are quickly filled with new sand. Our continuing life sooner or later begins to fill up the gap. Indeed, sometimes the hole fills up despite our valiant efforts to keep the walls surrounding our love's absence strong and sturdy. We try to build memorials to an absent love so that we can proclaim to the world: "I too once had a great love." Like the Walrus weeping copiously over the poor dead oysters in *Alice in Wonderland*, we weep over the death of our relationship ignoring the fact that if our love had stayed we would have eaten them alive. We weep copiously over a fictionalized memory of a great love which in truth is only half-remembered.

Such a separation "for good cause" may bring temporary anguish, but it cannot be compared with the grief that consumes us when a loved one dies. The young Augustine felt such heartache when he lost a dear friend to death. He was simply devastated. He writes:

> I was torn apart. I kept asking myself: "Why be sad?" But I had no answer. I told myself: "Hope in God!" but I could not because that dear human being, that friend who was now lost to me was more real to me than the vague image of God that I was supposed to hope in. My tears were my only delight now that my friend was gone (*Confessions*, 4.4).

The sorrow we feel when a loved one dies is indeed very profound and some never seem able to recover. But such grief is only natural. If we truly loved them, we *must* grieve when they leave us (*The City of God*, 19.8). Our only weakness is not that we loved them but that we loved them too extravagantly, loving them as though they would never die (*Confessions*, 4.7).

Still, all things considered, the pain that at times comes from having a passionate and deep love for another human is much less than the cheerless pain of those unhappy souls who have never experienced such love. Despite the tribulations that sometimes accompany our passionate affection, we still must give ourselves in love to others. Only thus can we begin to reach out to God. It is our love that draws us into our future and it is our innocent love of other humans that will draw us eventually into the arms of God.

6

The Need for Purification

1. Cleansing the Eyes of the Heart

In our search for the hidden God, we have at last come to the stage of final purification where we must cleanse the eyes of our hearts so that we can see the Lord when he comes. Finally discovering how to move beyond ourselves through love of others, we need now to move through that love to the love of God. To do this we must cleanse our eyes to see him; we must purify our love of others and overcome the "illnesses of the spirit" that hold us back.

But first we must cleanse our eyes. Augustine explains why this is necessary: "Having learned to love other human beings, you are ready to move to the next stage of your journey where you purge and clean out the eyes of your heart so that you are able to see God" (*On Christian Doctrine*, 2.7.11). This cleansing is needed not because our hearts have been especially dirty up to this point. If we have made some progress in the first five stages in our pursuit of God we have become fundamentally decent people. But we are not perfect and the residue of our past actions still clouds our vision. Our situation is not unlike what my eye doctor told me about my increasingly diminished vision. He said that I just had "old eyes," eyes that over time had accumulated a sludge that must be periodically washed away.

Augustine believed that the same sort of grime can dim the eyes of our hearts. The brilliance of God is in us and above us and below us and by our sides. The only reason why we cannot always see it is because the eyes of our hearts have become clouded, made opaque by cataracts growing on our spirit. As Augustine told his listeners:

> All of us want to see God and we are constantly searching for ways to see God. Indeed, sometimes we are on fire to see God. But scripture tells us that only the *pure of heart* will see God. For example, you are afraid to look at the sunrise when your eyes are blood-shot. The light of the rising sun is a joy to healthy eyes but it is a torment to eyes that are unhealthy. So too you cannot see with an impure heart what can only be seen with a pure heart (*Sermon 53*, 6).

The physical eye is made to be able to see the light of the sun but if irritating dust flies into it, it is cut off from that light. The obstacle must be removed for sight to be restored. Though the light is present to the eye, it nevertheless turns away because in its inflamed condition the light is painful. The same thing happens when the eyes of our hearts are diseased. We turn our backs on the Divine Light because we are too blind to see it or because looking at it is too painful. Looking at such divine brilliance becomes painful because we are forced to see how far we are away from the path to heaven, how empty our lives have become without some eternal root. So we look away, immersing ourselves once again in the pleasures of the moment, in the trivialities of day-by-day life, concerned only about "staying in shape" as though our shapely exterior can be made to last forever (*Sermon 88*, 5).

Augustine believed that the causes of the inflammation of our hearts' eyes are such things as greed, avarice, injustice, and, in general, lust for the things of this world. He added regretfully that while people quickly rush off to find a doctor if even a speck of dust clouds their sight, most seem unconcerned when the eyes of their hearts are damaged (*Sermon 88*, 6). Once such damage occurs, we imitate Adam after his fall from grace. In the beginning he rejoiced to walk arm and arm with God in Eden, but after his sin he dreaded to look at God's face. He fled into the darkness and the thickets of the woods, running away from the truth, clutching at shadows (*Sermon 88*, 6.). So too with us when the eyes of our hearts are clouded over. We continue to live in darkness or half-light because we are afraid to take the painful step of purification, a step that indeed can be painful because it demands a renewal of faith, a brave leap into the darkness, hoping that there is something beautiful out there to see although as yet we are unable to see it (*Sermon 53*, 10).

Only virtue will purify the heart but before it can enter we must sweep away the vices that stand in the way. Perhaps day by day we do not commit many grave sins but all of us accumulate the weight of small sins piled up over a lifetime. These must be drained out of our lives lest, like the sloshing bilge water in a small ship, they prevent our progress. As Augustine warned his friends:

> Sins, after all, are not just those that are called serious offenses, things like adultery, fornication, sacrilege, theft, robbery, false witness. These are not the only sins we commit. To pay attention to something you should ignore is a sin. To willingly listen to something perverse is a sin. To think evil thoughts is a sin. You object: "But my sins are little sins!" I answer: "How can they be little, if they can weigh you down and eventually bury you?" What is more tiny than drops of rain? But rivers are filled by them. What is more tiny than a grain of wheat? But granaries are filled with them. You protest that these little sins are not something to worry about. Do you not see how many there are? Try counting them and you will find out! (*Sermon 261*, 9-10).

Big or small, past or present, our sins have clouded over the eyes of our hearts. We must first cleanse those eyes before we can see the other areas of our lives that need purification. We must heed Augustine's wise advice: "Clean up your heart as much as you can! Work at it so that God may come and help you prepare the place where he wants to stay" (*Sermon 261*, 6).

2. Purifying Our Love

Since love is the energy that will eventually unite us with God and since our experience of love begins with our love for other human beings, we need to purify that love before we can achieve perfect love for God. It will not be easy. As Augustine said, "There is plenty of the wrong sort of love around and people are so filled up with the wrong sort that they can't develop the right sort" (*Sermon 368*, 3). It is sad that this is so because only the right sort of love can unite us to another human being or to God.

Loving other human beings is a precious blessing in this life, but there are many obstacles that must be overcome before it can become this "right sort" of love. Because we are "cracked" we have the tendency to "mess up" even the best of our human loves by our extreme selfishness. It is natural for us to "love" ourselves, but too much love for one's self stands in the way of any true love of others. Inordinate attention to self is the root of a destructive pride that makes us believe that we are better than everyone else, that we stand on the pinnacle of the mountain while others live out their lives in the mediocrity of the valley below. We become enraged when others do not seem to recognize our superiority. We are infuriated by the abject dumbness of those around us. Love them? They are lucky that we do not sweep them out of our way!

Sometimes the impediment that stands in the way of our loving others is that we are not loving them in the right way. For example, true love cannot exist:

1. When we desire another *as an object of pleasure*, desired only because they satisfy our physical or emotional needs.
2. When we desire another *as someone to dominate*, someone whom we can treat as a slave, in order to prove to the skeptical world that we are indeed a superior creation.
3. When we desire another *as a trophy or possession* to be displayed to an appreciative crowd so that they might marvel at such an extraordinary ornament being possessed by ordinary "clods" like us.
4. When we desire another *so obsessively* that we become incapable of loving anyone beyond them. Loving our human loves, we have no time or energy to love a Divine Friend.

Even when we avoid all these "wrong" sorts of love, our love can be weakened by envy or jealousy. We may become envious of the good things that draw us to our loved ones. Our loved ones have gifts that we would not dare to claim, and we wish that we had them. We wish that we were as smart or as good-looking or as popular as they are. The very good that makes us rejoice in them makes us sad when we look at ourselves. Nothing is more opposed to love than such envy (*Catechizing the Uninstructed*, 4.8). The reason is simple. The perfection of love is the *love of beneficence*, a love which wishes good for another because of the goodness that is in them. If we truly rejoiced in the good we find in our beloved, we would be happy even though we do not have their gifts. If we become envious of their special gifts, we may even begin to hate them. Rather than rejoicing in their good fortune, we are tormented by their well-being (*Sermon 353*, 1).

Another obstacle to true love is jealousy. When you are jealous of another, you see them receiving a good which you want exclusively for yourself. A lover may become jealous of other loving relationships that their beloved may have. A jealous spouse may become upset by any love not directed at themselves. They get angry when their partner is concerned about relatives, when they go out on the town with old friends, when the persistent demands of children take away the attention they believe should be showered on them. They may even begin to be jealous of God's love when they learn that it is shared equally by the whole human race. They seem to believe that love is a commodity destroyed by use, not something that is increased only by being shared with many others (*Commentary on the Letter to the Galatians*, # 52).

Such jealousy is destructive of love because at its root it is a lack of trust, that quality which is so essential for a true love of friendship. If our love is infected by a suspicion that our beloved is not totally committed to us, that their "sharing of hearts" with others somehow or other diminishes the share of their hearts that we have, then trust dies. Indeed, we may even begin to consider them as "the enemy" because we think that they have betrayed us by innocently loving another.

Love is also impeded when acquiring more and more *things* becomes more important than giving and receiving affection. For the acquisitive person, career becomes more important than family, the way family funds are spent becomes more important than nourishing a loving relationship. Disputes about money are frequently the cause of the anger and quarreling where the loving partners become unable to agree on how to spend the family's resources. Quickly the sharing of hearts dissolves into a controversy over "who gets what" and the principle of supposedly loving union becomes: "I got mine!" There is no longer any "ours."

Augustine maintained that there is not much we can do to eliminate anger from our lives just now (*Sermon 211*, 1). Our "cracked" condition and our infinite thirst for "good" sets the scene for rage when things do not go our way. In this imperfect life we can never get all the good things that we desire. We cannot always get those we love to love us in return. We cannot get those who do love us to love us with an exclusive love where we alone are the object of their affection. And, when we do not get what we want, we become angry. Worse still, when anger is nourished over time it festers and turns into hatred (*Commentary on Psalm 30*, 4). Such hatred is the ultimate impediment to loving humans or God. Hatred of God is what imprisons Satan in hell. Hatred of others makes real in us the somber declaration of Sartre that "hell is other people." Hatred is a darkness that completely eliminates the illumination that true love brings into our lives (*Commentary on Psalm 54*, 8).

To summarize, for love to be perfect we must love others for the good that we see in them. We neither abuse them or use them for our pleasure. We are not envious of the good we see in them nor are we jealous when we see that good being enjoyed by others. We do not become angry with them when they "impinge on our space" and above all we do not let anger blossom into hatred. If we can do all this, then indeed we have purified our love for each other and are prepared to reach beyond that love to love our still unseen God.

3. Curing Our Spiritual Illnesses

Having purified our ability to love, the next step in our purification is to conquer the spiritual illnesses that stand in the way of our progress. Using the analogy of a deer searching for the waters of a refreshing spring, Augustine advises:

> We should follow the example of the deer that destroys serpents that hinder its progress. After it kills these poisonous obstacles, its thirst for the refreshing brook-waters becomes even more intense. In our case, the serpents that stand in our way are the vices that sicken our spirit. How can we thirst for the spring when we are still filled with the venom of our vices? (*Commentary on Psalm 41*, 2-3).

Like the deer seeking the refreshing spring-waters described above, if we do not clear out the poisonous "serpents" that stand in our way, we will never be refreshed. We will never achieve the perfect happiness that comes with the vision of God.

The first of these "serpents" is *pride*. This is like a brain disease that causes us to develop the insane conviction that we are gods, that we are in charge of the universe, that we are in control of our lives, that we are more noble than the rest of the human race. This poisoned perception of reality causes us to look at the bed we have created for ourselves in this life and say, "My bed is my kingdom! There is nothing better in the universe!"

Pride is a difficult disease to overcome because we don't even know that we are sick, and we are deaf to any suggestion that we are. We pay no attention to the opinions of others because we don't think they have any worthwhile knowledge to communicate. We pay no attention to divine warnings because we are firmly convinced that we are God or at least as good as God. We are trapped in our own self-created imaginary heaven. We are not aware of being on a journey because we think we have arrived. We have no unsettling urge to move on. Indeed, even if we knew of God's kingdom in the distance, we could never get there because we are too swollen with our own importance to get through the narrow gate (*Sermon 142, 5*).

The second sickness that stands in the way of our progress is a form of heart failure. It is a *despair* that makes us give up on ourselves and on the grace of God. We are tempted to stay in the bed made for us by earthly fate, not because it is particularly satisfying but because we have no hope that we can ever get up. Why try to move if there is no hope for us in this life or in the next? The antidote for such despair is a careful listening to the loving words of Jesus and being surrounded by happy, hopeful friends. Of course, the grace of God is the one thing that is absolutely necessary but the workings of internal grace can be strengthened by the external grace of having others who are willing to listen to our sorrows and who try to move us to a happier frame of mind.

One of the positive effects of the intimate community of family and friends, is the presence of those who take a bright view of life, who do not *always* look for the down side of every day, who are not *always* negative about the human race, who (when surrounded by the dung of this world's stables) look happily for the hidden pony rather than complaining about the lack of maintenance. When surrounded by happy people, it is easier to be happy ourselves, or at least to wonder why we are still unhappy. Blessed indeed are those who do not live in the midst of "prophets of doom" because it is hard to see light when surrounded by the darkness of others.

The third disease that prevents our progress is the *cancer of malignant earthiness*. Its symptom is an overpowering attachment to things of this world, things that will necessarily pass in time. It is like the violent thirst that sometimes comes with physical illness but it is a very strange thirst indeed. It is a lust for more and more of what will inevitably become less and less. It causes a lassitude which makes us lie languidly in the bed we have made for ourselves in this life. We have no wish to ever move. We have no desire to experience anything beyond the peace that we can snatch from our here-and-now. Such earthiness carries with it the root of its own destruction. Sleeping in this earthly bed too long causes bedsores. The things we value in this life rust, wither away, or simply become boring. Sad to say, this world is just too limited to prevent the pallid "sameness" of even our most precious toys from eventually dimming their pleasure.

This cancer of earthly attachment manifests itself in various ways. If a person is infected with what the ancients called the *Concupiscence of the flesh*, they are turned "upside down" by their passionate desire for the good things of this life. That power (the spirit) that should be in charge becomes the slave to any and all desires for the material things of earth. When the pleasures and comfort of the body begin to dominate a person's life, the spirit which should be "on top" within the self now becomes the bottom. Augustine, no stranger in his youth to the "lusts of the flesh," later warned his friends about the disorder of such a life:

> How many evils are caused by the desire for pleasures of the flesh? Such wild, unrestrained desire results in adultery, fornication, drunkenness, and everything that unlawfully satisfies sensual needs. It invades the mind, leaving it enslaved by the flesh. It topples the ruler from its throne and subjects the master to the servant. How can humans act externally in an upright fashion when they have been turned upside down internally? (*Sermon 313a*, 2).

The answer is, or course, "They cannot!"

The second form of earthly attachment (*Concupiscence of the eyes*) disrupts our lives in quite a different way. It consumes us with an unhealthy curiosity. We peer into the lives of others hoping to find something strange or untoward, seeking pleasure in their excesses, excesses which of course we would *never* indulge in ourselves but which give us proxy pleasure when observed in others. Through persistent lust of the eyes we lose ourselves in the prurient or vicious games of others. Through our interest we identify with them. We lose ourselves in the frivolity of those around us and become in our imagination those whom we observe pursuing strange lives and performing stranger actions.

Finally, our attachment to this world may show itself in ambition, a *pride of life* which again causes our lives to become topsy-turvy by seeking immortality through our career and accomplishments. In desiring more and more earthly honors, more and more power over others, we begin to lose interest in anything beyond this place and this time. Human nature has as its goal eternal happiness beyond death, but the misdirected ambition of those infected with the "pride of life" is to be happy on earth with all the power and wealth and honor that they are able to achieve. They indeed live topsy-turvy lives because they have made their heaven on earth.

Augustine believed that pride and despair were the most dangerous diseases, but too much attachment to this world (in any of its three forms) is probably the most common. All three can prevent us from even beginning a search for God, trapping us in the little sick-beds we have made for ourselves. Only after having purified ourselves of these malignancies can we truly turn our focus to the heavens where the vision of God awaits us.

4. Purifying Our Focus

The final step in our purification is a change of focus from earth to heaven whereby we, finally free from the distractions of everyday life, are able to center our lives on our eternal destiny. If we can accomplish this, we will be ready to see God when and if he chooses to reveal himself to us. It is not an easy thing to do. Augustine writes that we humans are like ants crawling across a beautiful tile floor. We become so absorbed by the little piece of rock before us that we cannot see the beauty of the whole floor. And, as far as being able to raise our eyes to see the beauty above, that is just impossible! The task is beyond the capacity of our poor two-dimensional imagination (*On Order*, 1.1.2).

The warning conveyed by Augustine's analogy is that if we spend all our time focusing on every passing pebble in front of our noses, every fleeting event that momentarily catches our attention, we will never come to see the beauty of the universe. We will judge creation as a whole by the beauty or ugliness of the little piece of life we are living now, a practice which Augustine considers as absurd as judging the beauty of another by the attractiveness of their hair (*On True Religion*, 40.76). Focusing on these little bits of reality that fly past, we spread ourselves too thin. We rush about on the circumference of life. We "throw ourselves away" on every passing fancy (*Commentary on the Gospel of John*, 25.15.4) Cluttering our lives with more and more we become less and less. Our lives lose their center and we lose sight of the God who is at that center (*On Music*, 6.13.40).

Changing the focus of our lives does not mean that we ignore daily affairs. We must live out our lives in time on earth, crawling from day to day seeking what we need to get on with our lives. But if we attend to these passing needs in the right way, we still should have time to think of eternity. Living out our days in time, we should still be able to sense the presence of God in our lives, a firm underpinning for all we do. We begin to feel his presence like the throbbing sound of a bull fiddle giving substance to the fleeting melody of everyday life.

Augustine recognized that such focused attention is made difficult by the "bells and whistles," the "sights and sounds," of earthly diversions. As he wrote to a friend:

> Sometimes our spirits become so swollen with the joys of living on earth that we find it almost impossible to reflect on God. Indeed, I cannot help thinking that it would be easier to endure the violent storms of the wilderness than the turmoil we must suffer because or our daily involvement in the affairs of this world (*Letter 95*, 2 and 4).

There is nothing inherently evil in being interested in the affairs of this world. We humans have been given the great gift of being able to *wonder*, and through this gift we are able to appreciate the beauty of true art, to feel the thrill of competition, to experience the satisfaction of witnessing a difficult task done well. Such wonder at passing events becomes dangerous only when it prevents us from remembering where we are going. We become like the poor fellow on the superhighway, so intense in his gaping at the accident in the other lanes that he forgets where he is going and indeed even forgets that he himself is still rushing down a dangerous road. For him on the superhighway and for us on the road of life, such immoderate curiosity inevitably results in personal disaster.

Augustine believed that this was what happened to the Prodigal Son. The beginning of the boy's downfall was his overpowering curiosity about what the world "out there" was like (Luke 15:14-15), what answers were being given by astrologers, soothsayers, and secular masters to the mysteries of life. As a result:

> The son, torn away from his father (God) by the insistent hunger of his mind, began to feed on the husks of earthly teachings, husks which crackle and pop but do not satisfy, husks which are fit food for pigs but not for human beings (*Sermon 112a, 3*).

As long as the boy was consumed by curiosity about the husks of passing things, he was unable to appreciate the eternal.

To be honest, it seems quite easy to do. Such earthly "husks" are often less boring than discourses on heaven. Few fall asleep in a stadium while watching a football game; listening to a discussion of theology in a lecture hall leads to napping. Speaking from my own experience of teaching philosophy for forty years, I must confess that on some days I was more bored than my students. Even now, there are days when thinking and writing about spirituality loses out to fluffy TV presentations of the foibles and fables of the passing scene. On such days the description of the "dark night of the soul" seems less distressing than the dark screen of the broken cable TV.

Sometimes our curiosity leads us to spend hours peering into the lives of others, especially those odd people who surface on afternoon talk-shows. Consumed by interest in their strange problems, we have no time to devote to our own destinies, our own weaknesses, and strengths. As Augustine remarked: "We humans are sometimes hopeless creatures. The less we concentrate on our own faults, the more interested we become in the faults of others" (*Sermon 19*, 2–3).

It is probably because of our "cracks" that we have an almost irresistible temptation to focus on the foibles of others as we float past them on this river of time. Our own lives seem so dull by comparison and there seem to be so many truly outlandish things happening to others. As we merrily comment on the foundering lives of others, we cannot see that our own lives are in danger of sinking into the depths from all of the accumulated bilge-water of downright meanness that is ours alone (*Commentary on the Gospel of John*, 12.14.2).

Once our spirit has been truly purified, we will begin to acquire that simplicity of heart spoken of in Sacred Scripture where it tells us to seek God "in simplicity of heart" (Wis 1:1). Once we acquire such purity we will achieve a simplicity of focus whereby we can look for the God who is within, preferring him above all human loves and even our own selves. Suddenly our lives become uncomplicated. We begin to develop that "holy indifference" spoken about by the great mystics. We become able to subordinate desire for any person, place, or thing to our overwhelming confidence that God is guiding our lives. We stop worrying about losing things that are beyond our control and concentrate on the one and only thing that we *can* control: our salvation.

The more perfect our purification becomes, the more free we become to fly to the heavens. Like a balloonist, we cut the ropes holding us to the earth and begin to float higher and higher into the clear blue sky. We are still interested in the world below. Indeed, we look down upon it fondly. As our vistas expand with our increasing height, we are able to see more and more of this world and to understand our own little place in it. We have not rejected our friends, our work, our world, but we are no longer attached. We have acquired the freedom to "let them go" if it comes to that. Through our detachment, we are free to turn our faces to the heavens and to God. At last we are coming close to true wisdom and to being able to see the still hidden God when he passes by.

7

Loving a Still Hidden God

1. Climbing the Mountain

Three of the four Gospel writers tell the story of the first time human beings were called to ascend a mountain to *see* the transfigured Jesus-God. Matthew gives the following description of the event:

> Six days after his first prediction of his passion and death, Jesus took Peter, James and his brother John, and led them up a high mountain by themselves. There he was transfigured before them. And his face shone as the sun, and his garments became white as snow. And behold, there appeared to them Moses and Elias talking together with him. Then Peter addressed Jesus, saying, "Lord it is good for us to be here!" (Matt 17:1-4).

I have always felt that "climbing a mountain" is a fitting analogy for the story of our lives. All of us are searching for some "hill of transfiguration" and would dearly like to receive an invitation like the one given by Jesus to his three friends, the invitation to climb with him to the top of a mountain where finally we could see the glory that is God.

Some, like Albert Camus, were convinced that such a glorious mountain does not exist. The only mountain we have to climb in this life is the mountain of our daily tasks, a mountain that promises not glory but only frustration. We, like the doomed Sisyphus in the ancient myth, are condemned to push the rock of our burdens up the side of the mountain only to have it roll back down to the bottom at the end of the day, waiting for us to begin our struggles again the next morning. The crime of Sisyphus was that he tried to join with the gods; his punishment was an eternity of unending human labor.

Spiritual writers like Simone Weil, while recognizing the trials of our present life, remain optimistic. Certainly life for most ordinary humans has its fair share of suffering but such "affliction" can be a path to a better life. We are called upon to climb over the obstacles we find on this sometimes dark mountain of life, to climb past our own imperfections, in order to finally reach the heights where God waits for us to take us to our eternal home. Our task is to "climb up" so that eventually we might be "lifted up."

Augustine shares this optimistic view. Our search for the hidden God proceeds by ascending through intermediate steps of darkness, listening, discovery, bravery, human love, and purification. If we do this as best we can, then we may at last reach the "top of the mountain," that peak where we can patiently wait to be lifted up to an understanding of the wisdom that is God, perhaps for an instant to "see" the "face" of God.

Our desire for perfect happiness is in fact a desire for union with the infinite good that is God. We are built in such a way that we have a natural tendency to return to God because we have been made in the divine image. We are like boomerangs thrown into existence with an inherent need to return to the hand of our master. When we choose not to do so we whirl and twirl without roots through time and all eternity.

This desire for the infinite, this desire to be united with the transcendent is reflected in the psalmist's cry: "As the deer longs for the running waters, so my soul longs for you, O God" (Ps 42:2). Like a deer's thirst for water, we humans long for the nourishing fountains that can slake our thirst for happiness, the brilliant light that can illumine our darkened minds. The journey will not always be easy. Like deer in search for water, we may need to kill poisonous snakes (our vices) that block the way. Even in victory we must not rest on our laurels. We may have successfully cleared the path but we still have not arrived at our destination. We may have controlled our vices, but we have not yet reached the divine fountain that we need to refresh us. Until we do we must take Augustine's advice seriously: "When you judge yourself to be free of crooked desires, do not sit down as though you had nothing more to desire" (*Commentary on Psalm 41*, 3).

As we struggle to climb up the sometimes steep slopes of our lives, we should learn from the example of the deer. When crossing a raging river, deer will support each other through the dangerous waters (*Commentary on Psalm 41*, 4). We too can find support from others in our journey, encouraged by those faithful people who live lives of restrained desire, who like us are searching for truth, who endure bravely the harshness of life while being just and kind to others (*Commentary on Psalm 41*, 9).

We may become disturbed when others keep asking "Well, where *is* this God of yours?" It is a legitimate question and it has no good answer as long as we are still in the midst of our climb to the heights. It is no wonder then that we may sometimes be reduced to tears, but our faith makes them tears of anticipation. They are like the tears shed by a lover waiting impatiently for a loved one to arrive on an overdue plane. They are like the tears of children bursting with happy expectation as they stand before the "soon-to-be-opened" doors of an amusement park.

After a fruitless search to see the face of God in creation, I finally come to understand that the only place where I will be able to "see" God (and not simply believe in him) is not "around" me or even "in" me, but only *above* me. With one last great effort I struggle free of all that binds me to the dark valley below and reach the top of the mountain. There is no great feeling of accomplishment or pride. I have reached the top of the mountain of transfiguration, but God has not yet appeared. There is still a great distance between the top of my little hill and the place of God in the heavens.

Considering the space yet to be traveled to reach God's heaven, it becomes clear that I must remain humble if I am ever to make the trip. If I have achieved some sort of "holy peak" through my efforts at a virtuous life, it is only a little hill, and even this could only have been climbed with the help of God. I certainly cannot rely on myself to make the final leap into the heavens above, nor even to avoid falling once again into the darkness of the valley below. As Augustine says:

> I know that the Lord's righteousness abides, but whether my own will survive I do not know. The apostle's warning frightens me: "Anyone who thinks he stands must take care not to fall" (1 Cor 10:12). If I am satisfied with myself I will be displeasing to God (*Commentary on Psalm 41*, 12).

Only those who are not high and mighty can scale the slopes of daily life and then go beyond to that place where they may be granted the vision of the God (*Sermon 341*, 7). If I have succeeded in ascending the hill of transfiguration, I must be careful not to imitate the poor apostles who quickly fell asleep as soon as they reached the summit (Luke 9:32). I must remain prayerfully "turned towards God" as I wait patiently for the God who will someday come to take me the rest of the way home (*Commentary on Psalm 41*, 12).

2. Waiting on the Mountain

Shortly after Augustine's baptism, he and his mother apparently had an experience of the Divine Presence. They were waiting in a rented house in Ostia for a boat to take them back to their beloved North Africa, a trip that Monica was destined never to take (she died soon after). Augustine gives the following description of the ecstatic moment:

> A few days before my mother's death, the two of us were standing at a window and talking joyously about you, O God. As we continued to speak about your Divine Wisdom, our love flamed upward. With a final great leap of our hearts, we *experienced* your presence. This lasted only for an instant. Still elated by the memory, we returned to hear only the sound of our own voices (*Confessions*, 9.10.24).

For a moment Augustine and Monica were "lifted up" and given a "vision" of God. As far as we know, it was the one and only time that Augustine had such a mystical experience.

Such vision is indeed a special gift from God. There is nothing that we can do to force it. Assisted by the grace of God, we may have chosen to climb our own hill of transfiguration but there is no assurance that we will be "lifted up" any further. It is up to God to take us the rest of the way. There is no "ladder to God" that we can use nor is there a "tower of Babel" that we can construct that will take us to the heavens. Reaching the top of the mountain, all we can do is wait.

Simone Weil describes the need for such prayerful passivity as follows:

> There are people who try to raise their souls like a man continually taking standing jumps in the hopes that, if he jumps higher every day, a time may come when he will no longer fall back but will go right up to the sky. It is not in our power to travel in a vertical direction. But we need not search for God, only change the direction of our gaze. It is for him to search for us.[1]

Once reaching the top of the mountain of transfiguration, we must be quietly careful. We can still fall back by choosing the pleasures and comfortable certainties of the earthy life we have left behind. As Weil says, we must focus our attention on the heavens above, searching for the God who is now very near, waiting for him to "lift us up" to the place where we may glimpse him passing by.

This "vision of God" that we seek goes far beyond an "understanding of what God is" or a "getting a picture" from what others tell us. It is even more intimate and complete than the face-to-face contact we have with someone we love. Even if we are "two in one flesh," even if we have the most intimate physical union with our beloved, we still do not experience their "essence," that which makes them to be what they are. Our union with God goes far beyond that. It is more like the immediate awareness we have of our own "self," our own feelings, our own joys, our own fears, our own sorrows.

The vision of God promised in the next life and the mystical vision that is sometimes given in this life rests on an immediate contact with the very essence of Divinity. We do not become God but we do become one with God. This does not mean that we gain a full understanding or a full comprehension of the divine essence. God will remain a mystery even though we are united with him through all eternity. We will never completely comprehend the depths of that mystery. There will always be something new to amaze us (*Sermon 362*, 27–30). Our union with God in eternity will be like standing in the shallows of a vast ocean, joined to it but never able to plumb its depths.

Has anyone ever achieved this rapturous union in this life? Augustine believed that it was possible for anyone who has "died to this world" by purifying themselves of all earthy entanglements to be gifted with such vision (*Letter 147*, 13.31), and he was convinced that Moses and St. Paul actually received this gift (*The Literal Meaning of Genesis*, 12.27-28). However, this earthly vision will never have the perfection or permanence of the vision of God in heaven. Like Moses, the best we can expect to achieve is to see the "back parts" of a God who is quickly passing by (*The Literal Meaning of Genesis*, 12.27.55). The vision will be over before we know it and is not likely to change our lives that much.

Certainly, the vision of God did not solve all the problems that Paul and Moses faced during the rest of their lives. Paul was still afflicted by a "sting of the flesh" (2 Cor 12:8-9), and seeing God passing by did not prevent Moses from later distrusting him. At most, all such moments of ecstatic vision can do is to give a wonderful memory that may support hope as the trials and sorrows of this life continue.

We can only guess about how God "lifts up" his chosen friends from the summit of this earthly mountain to the glory of his heavenly house. Augustine hints that this final ascent from the summit will be accomplished in much the same way as we have been helped to reach the summit. We struggle to the heights by living a life of virtue and this is nothing else than (through the grace of God) loving in a proper way. We, like any creature capable of choosing between alternatives, can be influenced to act in a certain way by making us delight in one course of action rather than another. Augustine explains the process:

> Show a green branch to a sheep and you will attract it. Show a child some chestnuts and you will attract it. It is drawn by its love. It is drawn by desire of the heart. Now since it is true that every person is drawn by what pleases them, are we to say that Jesus-God cannot thus *draw* a person to Him? (*Commentary on the Gospel of John*, 26.6.5).

This image of "being drawn" is the one used by Augustine to describe the action of grace on the will as we strive to do those acts that will bring us to the summit of the mountain. Perhaps it is also the way that God will "lift us up" from the summit to see the home he has prepared for us. Augustine suggests that he may draw us by letting us hear the sounds of the party that is constantly going on in heaven:

> When people celebrate on earth, they usually set up musical instruments outside their houses or assemble singers or provide some kind of music which adds to the pleasure of the guests. If we are passing by and happen to hear it, we say, "What's going on?" And they tell us that it's some kind of party. Well, in God's home there is an everlasting party. Melodies from that eternal party reach and delight the ears of the heart. The sweet strains of that celebration drift into the ears of those who still walk on earth and they are drawn to the refreshing springs of water that eternally flow in heaven (*Commentary on Psalm 41*, 9).

Unfortunately, as long as we live on earth, the sounds and sights of heaven will never be so overpowering that we cannot ignore them. Even after a wonderful vision of God on the mountain, it is will be possible to fall back, to undergo a new darkness. We need caution as we wait patiently for God to come because if he does come to "lift us up," he will invite us so gently that we will always be able to close our ears to his invitation.

3. Falling Back

On the hill of transfiguration the three apostles (Peter, James, and John) had a brief vision of the glorified Christ. Peter never wanted the vision to end. He wanted Christ all to himself. He wanted to leave behind the dreadfully boring life of the valley below (*Sermon 78*, 3). But it was not to be. Christ was already on the way down from the summit, calling out:

> Come back down, Peter! You can't go on resting on the mountain. You must come down from your "high" to work again on earth. The people in the valley are waiting for you to love them and preach the truth to them. The security you seek now will be yours only in eternity (*Sermon 78*, 6).

After the vision was over and the three apostles had "come back down to earth," they must have wondered why it had happened. It certainly did not make their lives any easier. On Holy Thursday Peter would still deny Jesus three times; James would still run away, and John still would not have the stamina to do more than peek in from the edge of the crowd as his Lord was beaten, tried, and condemned.

There are important lessons in the story for us as we continue our own search for the hidden God. It teaches that after our laborious journey towards that place where we may finally expect to receive the gift of wisdom and the vision of God, we may be stuck in place waiting for an invitation to go higher, an invitation that may never come in this life. For most of us the story of our lives will not be a "being lifted up to the heavens"; it will be a "holding out for the Lord" (*Commentary on Psalm 26/2*, 23).

The story of the transfiguration also teaches us that even if we have been granted some sort of vision of God in this life, it will not last long. There may be a moment of ecstasy, but then it will pass. We will fall back to our ordinary life hoping that God will come again. But he may not. Indeed, like Sisyphus, we may be forced to begin our journey all over again, laboriously pushing our burdensome lives up to the heights once more. Both St. Paul and St. Augustine experienced such a fall from the heights. St. Paul had a vision he could not put into words but soon after he was given a thorn in the flesh, an angel of Satan to keep him from getting proud (2 Cor 12:7). St. Augustine speaks of a "trembling glance" by which he was able to discover God, only to be quickly brought back down to earth by his old habits (*Confessions*, 7.17.23).

Some who have been gifted with the experience of God fall back to a valley of darkness where God not only cannot be seen but seems to have disappeared entirely. This happened to St. Thérèse of Lisieux. After being bathed in the brilliance of Divine Light, she was plunged into darkness. She writes:

> God permitted my soul to be invaded by the thickest darkness, and the thought of heaven, up until then so sweet to me, became a cause of struggle and torment. It seemed to me that the darkness said mockingly to me: "You are dreaming about the light, about a fatherland embalmed in the sweetest perfumes. You are dreaming about the eternal possession of the Creator of all these marvels. You believe that one day you will walk out of this fog that surrounds you! Go forward and rejoice in a death which will give you not what you hope for but a night still more profound, the *night of nothingness.*"[2]

Some who fall back to the summit from being "lifted up" fall even farther because of their own bad choices. They embrace again the pleasures and addictions they had left behind. Once again they are dominated by lust for physical pleasure, by ambition, by an unhealthy curiosity about the world around them. They turn away from uplifting human love because of their renewed selfishness. They give in once more to the cowardice that had kept them from fighting their own passions, rejecting any thought of prayer for help, despairing of being able to deal honorably with the burdens of their lives.

Finally, they come to a point where they are not able to believe in anything. They remember their vision of the heavens as a fantasy. God has become for them a fiction; Christ, a historical figure of no great consequence. Once again they are a mystery to themselves. They close their ears to all advice because they believe that there is no one with the power or knowledge to point the way out of their darkness. Once living on the heights of wisdom, they have fallen in despair back to the darkness of the valley. Indeed, the darkness is now deeper than ever because there seems to be no room for hope. To those who tell them that the mountain is still there, that it is possible to climb again to the light of the summit, they sadly respond: "Been there, done that."

Why should this happen? Why should those who have been "lifted up" to the vision of God inevitably "fall back"? Why should so many God-fearing people be denied such vision? The first thing that needs to be said in answer to such questions is that no one is *owed* the vision of God. Even the reward of seeing God forever in the beatific vision is not something *owed* to us. It rests on a promise that God had no need to make. He could have created us and left us to get as much satisfaction out of this life as we could because there would be no life after death. Instead, he promised us immortality and (through his redemptive act of dying for us), he gave us the possibility of being undyingly happy.

It should come as no surprise that people who have achieved a brief vision of God in this life should "fall back" to their ordinary lives. For a brief moment they had lived in a world beyond their capacity and it was bound to end. The reason is simple. No matter how virtuous we become, we humans remain creatures of time, as of yet, incapable of functioning in eternity. We are still changeable creatures, incapable of standing immobile for long even before the face of God. We are *in time*, not yet *in eternity*. Moreover we are still "cracked," subject to the temptations, weakness, and maladies that are part of our fallen state. As a result:

> First dazzled by the intuition of God as light and truth, we fall back. We are dragged down by the filth of clinging passions and by the confused wandering that is common to our exiled state (*On the Trinity*, 8.2.3).

We may have been redeemed but we have not yet been fully healed. We now get "sick and tired" physically and sometimes get "sick and tired" of being good. St. Paul had his "sting of the flesh"; St. Thérèse had her pain of physical illness; St. Augustine had his fragile health and these afflictions would never disappear as long as these saints lived on earth (*Commentary on Psalm 106, 7*).

We should not be distressed if we have tried our best to climb the mountain of transfiguration and are still waiting to be "lifted up." There can be a certain peace in such patient waiting. We have done all we can. It is up to God to move us farther. Having purified ourselves (as best we can) of earthy desires, we can now discover the final freedom, the *freedom from the necessity of choice*. No longer must we make critical decisions about our future (beyond resisting the temptation to go back). We stand quietly. Our destiny is now in the hands of someone else who will decide when and where we shall go and how we shall get there. We stand free before the providence of God.

Like a little baby clutching the leg of its mother, we stand and wait to be carried, realizing that there is now nothing we can do to determine our future. We are free and can sit back and wait for our future to unfold, convinced now of the wisdom expressed by an old friend of mine (in the early stages of Alzheimer's disease) that "things must be some way" and there is nothing we can do to change the way things "will be." We are like those patient folks described by Simone Weil:

> They do not turn toward God. God himself sets their faces in the right direction. It is for them to remain motionless, without averting their eyes, listening ceaselessly, and waiting. If after a long period of waiting God allows them to have an indistinct intuition of his light or even reveals himself in person, it is only for an instant. Once more they have to remain still, attentive, inactive, crying out only when their desire cannot be contained.[3]

Is it possible to still have joy while waiting for God to come and "lift us up"? The answer must be "Yes." There is a quiet joy possessed by all good people who have tried their best to climb the mountain from darkness to wisdom by living a decent life. It is a peace that comes from a hope expressed by Augustine in the question: "Will he who gave so great assurances while I was on my journey abandon me on my arrival?" (*Commentary on Psalm 26/2*, 10).

4. The Wisdom of Those Who Wait

If we have been lucky enough to have received a momentary vision of God but have now come back down to earth or if we have never received such a vision, our dilemma is: "What am I supposed to do now?" Somehow or another I must love God if I am to be drawn towards him as my ultimate end but how can I do this if he is unseen? It is a crucial question for those of us who are still struggling to master the early stages of the climb to wisdom. Perhaps we have come to some sort of love for others and even have to some extent withdrawn ourselves from earthly attachment. But few of us would dare to claim that we have yet achieved wisdom, that we have reached the summit where God may reveal himself. We may have some sort of an awareness of God as we struggle through life but few experience even the momentary ecstasy of vision. How can we truly "love" this God who is still hidden and will likely remain hidden on this side of death?

The solution to our problem is to turn our love towards those whom we *can* see, those with whom we share humanity. Augustine puts it this way:

> How should we prepare for loving God? By loving each other! You may say to me, "I have not seen God." Can you say to me, "I have not seen a human being?" Love each other! If you love the human whom you see, you will love God too at the same time; for you will see love itself, the love that is the God who dwells within each of us (*Commentary on the Epistle of John, 5.7.2.*)

If we are able to love others with some degree of unselfish love, a pure love not dictated by our own self-love, then we are at least *beginning* to love God through them. This is the clear message the apostle John sent to his followers:

> We must love one another because love is a gift of God. Anyone who loves is a child of God and has some experience of God. True, no one has ever seen God but if we love one another, God lives in us. God *is* love and anyone who lives with love lives in God and God lives in them. If you do not have love for the neighbor that you can see, you cannot love the God who is not yet seen. Thus, the command we have received from God is simply this: if you say you love God, you must also love your neighbor (1 John 4:7-21).

But who is our neighbor? As the parable of the Good Samaritan (Luke 10:30-37) makes clear, our neighbor is every human being, especially those who need our help. The Samaritan who rescued the injured man from the ditch was a stranger, an alien, an enemy in the eyes of the culture of that time and place. Yet he reached out in love to someone he did not know simply because he was a human and as such was a "neighbor." We must go out in love to these other humans if we are ever to discover God. Our love for these human loves is like the hand of the soul. In holding onto them, we are holding onto the place of God; in loving them with a pure selfless love we are establishing the conditions for coming to a pure love of God.

If we are lucky, we may find someone who shines with a visible spark of the divine. God's home is in heaven but here on earth he has a place in the hearts and souls of those devoted to him. They are God's "tent" in this land of pilgrimage. In our admiration for and love of the good people we find around us on our own journey, we can be refreshed and encouraged to go farther (*Commentary on Psalm 26/2*, 6). "Living saints" (people like Monica and Ambrose and Simplicianus and Ponticianus) certainly played a major part in Augustine's conversion. He was able to see in these human "tents" or "places" of God the hint of the wonder of God himself. As he would later remark: "God's home on earth is found in those who are faithful to him" (*Commentary on Psalm 41*, 1).

Through our love for the good people that we have come to love, through our wonder at their faith-filled lives, we begin to hope that there is indeed something and someone above us who will make sense out of our absurd lives, someone who will accept us despite our confusion, someone who loves us despite our unbelief. Indeed, in loving the lovely people who run with us through life, we experience the love of God without being conscious of it. It is this invisible divine love that has brought us together with all those whom we have loved and still love. It is this divine love that has enabled us to rejoice not in our own "selves" but in the wondrous selves of our loved ones. As Simone Weil wrote: "Nothing among human things has such power to keep our gaze fixed ever more intensely upon God than friendship for the friends of God."[4]

Even though we cannot see the God of love, at least our love can be focused on the neighbor that we can see, doing those pedestrian things we can sometimes do for those we care about. If we cannot feel the love of God, at least we can be *kind* to each other. Such was the conclusion reached by St. Thérèse of Lisieux when at the end of her life she no longer could sense the intimate presence of God. Mary Frohlich describes this period in Thérèse's life as follows:

> Feeling herself at an immeasurable distance from God, she abandoned herself to letting God love through her all those who are "nothing." She shifted her attention from desire for a heaven "elsewhere" to a passion to be involved in, to throw herself into the present moment, a moment composed only of love. She no longer expected to encounter the "essence" of God. Instead she dedicated herself to simply living neighborly charity in the ordinary "here and now."[5]

There is always *something* that each one of us can do for those we meet on our pilgrimage to heaven. As Augustine told his parish congregation:

> We should all do for one another whatever things we have at our disposal. If you have more than enough, lavish it on those

with little or nothing. Let those with money feed the poor, clothe the naked. Let those with the gift of counsel guide others by scattering the darkness of doubt with the light of a loving faith. If others can teach, let them distribute truth from the storehouse of the Lord, confirming the faith of the faithful, calling back those who stray, seeking out the lost. There are things that even the poor can do for each other. They can loan their feet to the lame, the use of their eyes to the blind. Some can visit the sick; others can bury the dead. Indeed, it is extremely difficult to find anyone who cannot do something for someone else. As St. Paul says: "Bear one another's burdens and in this way you will accomplish the law of Christ" (Gal 6:2) (*Sermon 91*, no. 9).

At very least by lovingly serving others here on earth we prepare ourselves to love the God whom we will eventually see. In loving others we can come to know something about God. Even though the best we can achieve is to see "the back parts of God," it is a beginning (*The Trinity*, 2.17.28). Even such imperfect awareness of the Divine will make this life a bit more bearable. The darkness in which we began our journey will clear and our hope will strengthen, the hope that some day we will reach the land of eternal life where finally we will see God face-to-face. In the meantime we are at peace. We now know that we are not alone. We are surrounded by those we love. We are accompanied by the still hidden God who lives in them and who will stay close to us as we journey on through all the rest of the days of our lives. When we reach out to others in love, we make true for ourselves the happy fact preached so long ago by Augustine: "Wherever you go on earth, however long you remain, the Lord is close to you. So don't worry about anything. The Lord is always nearby" (*Sermon 171*, 5).

Notes

1. Simone Weil, *Waiting For God*, Emma Crauford trans. (New York: Harper-Colophon Books, 1973) 194, 216.

2. John Clarke, O.C.D. (trans), *Story of a Soul: The Autobiography of St. Thérèse of Lisieux*, 3rd ed. (Washington, D.C.: ICS Publications, 1996) 211–13.

3. Simone Weil, *op. cit.*, 211.

4. Ibid, 74.

5. Mary Frohlich, H. M., "Desolation and Doctrine in Thérèse of Lisieux," *Theological Studies*, vol. 61 (2000) 270, 274.

Epilogue

The seven stages in the ascent to the vision of God are not mutually exclusive. In the midst of the ecstasy of human love there may be fear. If we have scaled the heights to the place where God dwells, we still may suddenly be enveloped in darkness. For most of us, all of the stages may well be mixed together as long as we live, a succession of rising to the top of the mountain of transfiguration and falling again into the dark valley below.

The hope-filled message of faith is that God is already present in us if we are trying to deal with whatever stage is ours at the moment: hoping in darkness, listening with an open mind, learning with humility, praying bravely, loving others unselfishly, purifying our desires unwaveringly, patiently waiting for the still unknown God to come. Any and all of these noble acts would be impossible without the support of God's uplifting grace illuminating our minds and strengthening our will.

We may never achieve any direct vision of God in this life, even if we have been able to struggle to the top of the mountain by living decent lives as best we could. We may never be "lifted up." We may never see the vision of the glorified Christ that was given to the three apostles on the hill of transfiguration. Does this mean that we have not received the gift of wisdom? The answer is "No." It just means that wisdom must manifest itself in us through our patient acceptance of God's will.

It is consoling to realize that the guarantee that we shall eventually see God for all eternity is not based on whether or not we have had some mystical experience of him in this life. Rather it is determined by our continuing struggle to be worthy to receive this vision, by our struggle to keep our focus on what is above rather than what is below, by our continuing struggle against the temptation to turn back in despair.

We prepare to see and love God by trying to live a decent life and it is these efforts that insure our salvation. A mystical experience of God, a vision of God, an overpowering feeling of love for God, all of these are gifts that God may (or may not) give to us. The gift that we give to him is our effort to scale the mountain. It is up to him to take us the rest of the way and he may not do that until the moment of our deaths. Indeed, we may never get much beyond the first stage, the darkness of not-knowing. Only after death will all darkness dissipate. Only then will we realize that we have been saved by our own efforts and God's grace, not by moments of ecstatic vision granted to us in this life.

I have never seen the hidden God, but the words of the saints of the past and the experience of the saints of the present have given me hope and in that hope I find the beginning of happiness. Like the little "Donald-child" waiting for the father to start the family car for the trip to the seashore, I am happy anticipating the sweetness of the endless ice cream that is sure to come.

CPSIA information can be obtained at www.ICGtesting.com
Printed in the USA
LVOW082104151211

259660LV00001B/7/P

9 780814 629574